Nurturing
Young Children's
Disposition
to Learn

Nurturing Young Children's Disposition to Learn

Sara Wilford

Redleaf Press®
www.redleafpress.org
800-423-8309

Published by Redleaf Press
10 Yorkton Court
St. Paul, MN 55117
www.redleafpress.org

First edition 2009
Cover design by Lightbourne
Cover photograph by Vadim Ponomarenko
Interior typeset in Minion and designed by Erin New
Interior photos by Margery B. Franklin
Printed in the United States of America

16   15   14   13   12   11   10   09   1   2   3   4   5   6   7   8

Library of Congress Cataloging-in-Publication Data
Wilford, Sara.
    Nurturing young children's disposition to learn / Sara Wilford.
        p. cm.
    Includes bibliographical references.
    ISBN 978-1-933653-47-1
1. Early childhood education. 2. Learning. 3. Early childhood teachers—
In-service training. I. Title.
    LB1139.23.W56 2009
    372.21—dc22
            2008030720

FSC

Recycled
Supporting responsible
use of forest resources

Cert no. SW-COC-002283
www.fsc.org
© 1996 Forest Stewardship Council

Printed on 100% postconsumer waste paper

For Ronald

Nurturing Young Children's Disposition to Learn

Foreword

During the past two decades, the standards movement has gained tight control over education in the United States. Schools have raised academic demands and have made standardized testing the centerpiece of the school year. What's more, the standards movement has steadily moved down to very young ages. Today even kindergarten, once a playful introduction to school, is largely academic, and many kindergarten classes assign homework. Standardized testing, too, has become increasingly prevalent in kindergarten and the first two elementary grades. And now there is a growing call for academic preschools so children will be prepared for the rigors of kindergarten.

One would be hard-pressed to say the standards movement has improved the nation's academic achievement. Nevertheless, it certainly has affected children. To prepare children for the tests, teachers have been forced to sacrifice many activities that children find stimulating and rewarding, such as the arts, creative projects, and classroom discussions. Many school districts have even eliminated recess. Students find the heavy diet of test-prep drills and exercises dreary and tedious—a tedium that turns into fear as the testing dates approach.

Despite these ill effects, resistance to the standards movement has been sporadic. To be sure, some parents and students have protested against excessive testing, but the protests have been few and far between. Some public officials have criticized a cornerstone of the standards movement—the federal No Child Left Behind (NCLB) law—but the criticisms have mostly focused on technical and funding issues, not the way NCLB affects children. One might have expected teachers to revolt against so much test-driven education, but so far their opposition has lacked force.

Yet I predict that as the standards movement continues to expand into the young ages, opposition will mount. Standards advocates push for more academic instruction, but eminent educators like Sara Wilford show that it's especially misguided to approach young children as if they were merely rational intellects. Before the age of seven years or so, children learn largely through play, the senses, and physical, social, and artistic activities. They learn best when they feel valued in a warm and nurturing environment. And while young children do begin to pick up some academic concepts, they do so in their own ways and at their own pace—not according to uniform testing timetables.

Wilford, who directed the Early Childhood Center at Sarah Lawrence College for twenty years, brings deep insights to early childhood education. She draws upon recent research and innovative approaches. As she offers new ideas and suggestions, she is never talking just about test scores or mental abilities; she is always talking about a real child, with a full range of emotions and creative capacities, as well as a distinctive family and cultural background.

Early in this book, Wilford tackles one of the central questions in contemporary early education: How important is make-believe play? Many education officials consider make-believe play to be frivolous, and preschools and nursery schools are pushing it aside to make more room for academic instruction. But Wilford shows that pretend play is vital to the child's development; it is a principal means by which a child develops the capacity to think in symbols. When a child pretends that a crayon is a hypodermic needle and gives her doll a "shot," the crayon serves as a symbol. Because children spontaneously invent and value symbols, they will readily appreciate how the marks called letters and words can be symbols too. Moreover, make-believe play fosters children's imaginative powers, and as children create increasingly elaborate dramas, they develop the capacity for joyful persistence.

Wilford wants children to develop their unique strengths. She recommends Howard Gardner's theory of multiple intelligences as a guide to individual talents, and she shows how teachers can nurture these talents while also helping individual children stretch into other areas. For example, one child is encouraged to develop his exceptional math skills through individualized work, but he also is encouraged to extend his ability to block play so he can collaborate with other children and develop his social intelligence. Other children are fidgety in class, but focus intently during the games on the playground. Wilford wants teachers to nurture these children's physical talents while looking for ways to extend them to a wider range of class activities.

Throughout this book, I was struck by Wilford's emphasis on the positive. She clearly loves children and wants us to appreciate every single child. She wants all children to succeed—not in the limited sense of high test scores, but in the development of their full potentials.

William Crain
Professor of Psychology
The City College of New York

Acknowledgments

Looking back over the course of my career in education, there are many people to whom I am indebted. First and foremost, thanks to my husband, Ronald Wilford, who sent me back to school and encouraged me at every point along the way by asking, "Do you really want to do this?" followed swiftly by "Then, DO it!"

Thank you to many gifted friends and educators, particularly Sarah Lawrence College Early Childhood Center teachers past and present and Director Lorayne Carbon. I am also grateful to Director Elaine Karas and the talented teachers at Purple Circle Early Childhood Program and Parent-Cooperative in New York City for sharing their wisdom and perspectives on documentation; to Yvette Richardson for her sensitive reading of and content suggestions for chapter 2 on changing families, societal challenges, and cultural differences; to Patricia Carini for her encouragement and reading of chapter 5 on Prospect Center's descriptive processes; and to my Art of Teaching, Child Development Institute, and psychology faculty colleagues at Sarah Lawrence College for their never-ending support.

Special thanks go to Margery Franklin for her enthusiasm and her beautiful photographs of children and early childhood environments, which add significant dimension to the text. Bill Crain's wisdom and encouragement, and his generous foreword to this book, are deeply appreciated.

And to David Heath, editor-in-chief at Redleaf Press, who has been a joy to work with at each stage of the development of this manuscript.

Finally, my special gratitude goes to all the children who have enriched my life and work. They have nurtured my own disposition to learn.

Introduction

For a long time I have been interested in the word "disposition." I am particularly interested in two closely linked ways of thinking about the meaning of disposition as it relates to young children and learning. First, a child's disposition indicates his or her individual approach, temperament, and range of interests. Disposition in this case may be thought of as learning style, or as the particular set of strengths with which each child approaches the world. For example, some children are by nature reflective, others outgoing, and still others a combination of contemplative and sociable. Yet all are involved in the active process of making sense of their daily experiences. A second, equally important aspect of disposition is the child's disposition *to* communicate, explore, and learn. Early childhood author and educator Lilian Katz (1987, 153) writes about this meaning of disposition in the following way. "*Dispositions,* usually omitted from lists of educational goals, are broadly defined as relatively enduring habits of mind, or characteristic ways of responding to experience across types of situations, for example, curiosity, generosity, . . . and so on." She adds, "One of the important dispositions of concern to educators of young children is their *interest,* or their capacity, to lose themselves in an outside activity or concern. Interest refers to the ability to become deeply enough absorbed in something to pursue it over time and with sufficient commitment to accept its routine as well as its novel aspects" (158).

This book will take into account young children's individual dispositions while focusing on specific ways that early childhood teacher-caregivers can use their knowledge of each child in their classrooms to foster the disposition to learn. Child development experts and early childhood educators have long endorsed the well-established principle that social and emotional factors are inseparably connected to cognitive growth. New Zealand educator Marie Clay puts it this way:

> A child starting school does so with mixed feelings and some misgivings. Security, self-confidence, acceptance, and a sense of belonging are a foundation for attitudes that encourage participation in effective learning experiences. Happy, relaxed, stimulating relationships between children and between child and teacher promote growth of personality which in turn advances achievement. (Clay 1991, 40)

Neither Katz nor Clay is advocating for an absence of teacher input. They echo Lev Vygotsky's belief in a zone of proximal development for which effective teachers are alert, watching for signs of the child's interest, as they support and respond to a need for assistance or the introduction of new material (Crain 2005, 239–40). Thus, early childhood teacher-caregivers can be confident that when children are responded to and valued for who they are and how they think, both developmentally and as unique persons, their self-esteem and natural curiosity will flourish and become springboards to skill development and genuine inquiry.

Part 1 of this book, "Perspectives on Learning," sets a framework that is both theoretical and accessible. Directors of early childhood programs may use each chapter in part 1 as a staff development tool, one that enriches teacher-caregivers' own knowledge and empowers them in their conversations with parents. Chapter 1 begins with a basic description of the developing brain, confirming that all healthy children enter the world ready to learn. By exploring recent advances in brain research and investigating the process of synapse development, we see that learning is not a process of "cramming in," but rather one that involves the child absorbing and eventually pruning information derived from experiences. Thus, scientific findings that show the importance of children learning in the context of significant relationships—in environments that promote their self-esteem and their disposition to inquire and discover—validate established theories that influence early childhood education practice such as the developmental-interaction approach. A description of the developmental-interaction approach, conceptualized and refined at the Bank Street College of Education, demonstrates how nurturing all aspects of young children's growth—social, emotional, and intellectual—fosters positive outcomes through interactions with others and with materials that characterize effective learning environments.

Chapter 2 reflects on changing families, societal issues, and cultural differences through the identification of some major challenges faced by early childhood teacher-caregivers and directors today. These challenges are often overlapping, as they include the many variations in family makeup, economic status, and cultural background that comprise our richly diverse society. Understanding the context of children's lives is a complex yet essential task for educators of all children.

Chapter 3 examines Howard Gardner's multiple intelligences theory, illustrating how a renowned developmental/neuropsychologist has framed an understanding of intelligence that makes visible the often-ignored manifestations of intellectual power in appreciation of children's individual expressions of intelligence. Examples of persons who have demonstrated their specific expressions of intelligence are placed side by side with examples of children whose behaviors may alert teachers to individual dispositions and strengths.

Part 2, "Perspectives on Practice," begins with chapter 4, which describes my 1993 visit to the schools of Reggio Emilia, Italy, and the effects of that visit. This was an inspirational experience that led me to think about learning environments in a new way. Bringing these experiences back to my own program resulted in aspects of change and the appreciation of change as an ongoing ingredient of vibrant early childhood practice. The various sections of this chapter address

- room arrangement

- dramatic-play areas

- classroom libraries

- range and accessibility of art materials

- open-ended materials, both classic and collections of found materials for construction

- materials that appeal to the senses, for example, cooking, sand and water play, playing musical instruments

- embedded literacy and numeracy activities that become part of daily choices

The concept of emergent curriculum, embracing the Reggio Emilia approach and Lilian Katz's project approach, focuses on the development of young children's skills and knowledge alongside their dispositions and emotions. As taught in the Art of Teaching program at Sarah Lawrence College, emerging projects are viewed as entry points through which all children can find ways to make meaning.

Observation skills are essential for all of us who work with young children. Chapter 5 outlines a descriptive review process, developed by Patricia Carini at the Prospect Center in Vermont. The Descriptive Review of a Child is both a specific and a reflective approach to observation. It is accessible and immensely useful for both directors of early childhood programs and teacher-caregivers. This powerful tool also helps parents understand that the school really knows their child as a person. It serves as a vehicle for parents and others on the school staff to contribute to a rounded, informed view of each child as an individual.

Chapter 6, "Developing Positive Communication," begins with a discussion of finding your own voice as an effective teacher as you assess the roles of trust, tone, and structure in providing for the needs of every child in your class. This chapter looks at

- group interactions

- ways in which children's ages and temperaments affect communication

- the often overlooked importance of nonverbal communication

- the possibilities for and benefits of multi-age grouping (three to five years)

Essential aspects of communication between teacher-caregivers and families are explored in the context of a full-day program, from morning drop-off to evening pickup, including techniques for dealing with separation and the more relaxed, transitional, late-day needs of children and staff.

Chapter 7 highlights the National Association for the Education of Young Children's (NAEYC) summary of early learning standards, while addressing the often-overlooked fact that children hold standards for themselves. Authentic assessments emphasize the value of observation, longitudinal records, and collecting children's work over time. These dynamic assessment tools help parents experience their children's progress. Keeping individual differences in mind, this chapter's review of curriculum contains a focus on early literacy, beginning with the importance of pretend play in developing symbolic processes. This chapter

- describes the progression from pictures to words

- identifies opportunities for phonological awareness

- acknowledges the illogical nature of English spelling

- explains the value of experimenting with inventive spelling as an important step toward the conventional

- puts handwriting in perspective

Literacy is described within the context of the classroom community, including interactive, "solo," and group times. The teacher's role emerges as that of coach and leader as she reads to and with children, writes down their very own words that can be read back, and engages them in songs, rhymes, and word analysis as their skills progress.

In conclusion, chapter 8 endorses the warm interactions and frequent communications that help teacher-caregivers encourage parents to appreciate and build on their children's unique strengths. Parents today are anxious about their children's progress, so adequate conference time is needed to set a positive tone and create an open dialogue. Conference time can be used to interpret progress as encompassing the interlocking avenues of developmental growth described in chapter 1. This final chapter also includes tactics for

- maintaining structure within a specified conference time limit

- explaining the school's philosophy and assessment strategies

- demonstrating individual strengths and growth by presenting sequential examples of a child's work

Chapter 8 also includes suggestions on how to react to challenges from parents who question the value of imaginative play, a developmental approach to literacy, and the place of technology in early childhood classrooms. Suggestions for parents emphasize the value of building strong vocabularies and thinking skills for second-language learners by conversing in their home language(s), and the importance of parents' reading aloud, telling stories, and sharing rhymes in interactive rather than instructional ways. Additional suggestions include helping parents recognize their child's reading behaviors, finding opportunities to write down the child's words, and keeping appropriate reading and writing materials available. Without overwhelming already stressed parents, teacher-caregivers can assure families that normal home routines and opportunities for unstructured play are still essential elements for developing a child's social, emotional, and intellectual growth.

Part 1

Perspectives on Learning

Nature and Nurture, Social Issues,
and Individual Dispositions

Chapter 1

Brain Research and the Learning Child

Walking into a classroom of young children never fails to energize me. In classrooms designed for engagement and motivation, I am always thrilled to observe children's enthusiasm, to feel their investment in experimentation and discovery. I can honestly say that I have learned the most about my work as an early childhood teacher, center director, and teacher educator from observing and listening to individual children in the process of their growth and development.

This is an exciting time for teachers, caregivers, and directors. Scientific discoveries are supporting insights about the developing child that early childhood educators and psychologists have long understood from their observations of children. Nurturing young minds and spirits, in effect nurturing all aspects of the whole child, can never again be seen as a "fuzzy" or "soft" approach to early childhood education. Strong evidence also supports the idea that children's intelligence manifests itself through a range of pathways, thus mandating all who work with young children to view them through their strengths rather than their perceived weaknesses. We must remember that the IQ tests frequently chosen to evaluate our youngest have a high rate of unreliability (Heubert and Hauser 1999, 279). For the above reasons, this chapter will use the lens of brain research as a means of validating a respected developmental approach to early childhood education.

Brain Research: Nature and Nurture

With the advent of sophisticated brain imaging, studies increasingly relate scientific findings to implications for the care and education of young children. This is important research, and mounds of new information will become available in the years ahead. However, perhaps the most relevant aspects of brain research for early childhood professionals lie in the support they provide for knowledge based on observations of young children by psychologists and educators over many previous decades. One aspect of these observations, supported by brain research, can now be considered a truth: both nature (the child's genetic makeup) and nurture (the child's unique experiences) are equally central to healthy growth and development in the early years. This has implications not only from birth to age three, but throughout childhood.

The brain controls literally all of our physical and intellectual functions, processing information both past and present as it continuously responds and adapts. A few irrefutable scientific facts can be helpful in understanding how the young child's brain develops:

- A newborn's brain contains as many brain cells—one hundred billion—as an adult's, but the baby's brain cells (or neurons) are not yet wired to form neural pathways that have gone through a process of fine-tuning.

- A baby's brain cells begin to grow "signal-senders" called axons and dendrites. The axon of one neuron attaches itself to another neuron's dendrite to form a connector called a synapse that is energized by electrical impulses (or neurotransmitter chemicals) within the neuron or brain cell.

- Synapses allow information to travel from one part of the brain to another. Through a combination of genetic and environmental input, they increase at an amazing rate so that a three-year-old child's brain can be expected to have 1,000 trillion synapses—or about double those of an adult.

- For the first ten years of life, another process goes on that is sometimes called "pruning" or "fine-tuning." This happens when a piece of information or a stimulus becomes unnecessary and the synapse is sloughed off. So although the density decreases, the brain's information becomes more hardwired.

One issue that has emerged, amid increased understanding of the young brain's capacity, relates to the knowledge that immense learning possibilities are inherent in the first three years of life. This does *not* mean, however, that babies' heads should be crammed with information during this time. Some researchers prefer thinking about development from birth to age three as a "sensitive" period, rather than a "critical" period, and draw attention to the fact that the child's environment, the comfort and encouragement she or he receives from nurturing caregivers, coupled with an understanding of the brain's ability to adjust and reorganize, are far more important factors than any direct teaching could be.

All of us who work with young children—in early childhood centers, preschools, Head Start programs, and other early childhood settings—are keenly aware of the importance of consistency in our work. Primary caregiving calls for the very youngest to be nurtured by the same caregiver on a regular basis. Consistent teachers and their assistants provide ongoing security to three-, four-, and five-year-olds. This consistency is important not only for children, but for the families with whom we partner. It builds trust. The journal that travels back and forth between the caregiver or teacher and the home can convey important information for parents to respond to about

- that first tooth

- that first step

- a photo of the birthday celebration

- a note that just says, "I love you so much I needed to give you a special hug today!"

Your sensitivity helps allow parents to share developmental milestones that happen when their children are with you. Suggestions such as "You might want to rub Jenna's gum where she usually puts her teething ring," or "Matt seemed very close to taking a step on his own today" erase competition and empower parenting. Barbara Bowman uses the term "responsive care" to emphasize the relationship between teacher-caregivers' nurturance of individual children and their ability to learn. "Finding out what and how much children need, and providing it, is one of the most important challenges for teachers and caregivers, and when that happens, children are open to a variety of experiences from which they can learn" (Bowman and Moore 2006, 53).

Brain development can also be affected by negative experiences of an environmental nature. The Austrian psychoanalyst Dr. René Spitz made an early black-and-white film to demonstrate his research on the importance of infant-adult attachment. The goal was to show that emotional development, nurtured by human warmth and engagement, is tied to intellectual and physical development. He observed and followed the progress of children, infants to two-year-olds, in two institutional settings in the late 1930s and 1940s. One of the settings was a prison nursery where mothers were allowed to play with their own babies, to converse with other inmate mothers, and to interact with other inmates' babies as well. In this nursery, one-year-olds vocalized, walked, and climbed around with curiosity as they interacted with people, objects, and toys. The other setting was an orphanage caring for forty-five babies who were looked after by five nurses. These babies received good health care in sanitary conditions. They were changed and fed on a regular basis. In the film, Dr. Spitz approaches an infant who appears to be about six months old and is propped in the corner of a crib. The doctor coos and cajoles, trying to make eye contact. He smiles and wiggles his fingers, finally picking up the limp infant from the crib. The infant is, in fact, not six months, but two years old. Dr. Spitz's voice-over tells us that many of the children in this nursery failed to thrive, were considered to be seriously retarded, and often died.

At the time, Spitz's work was criticized as perhaps being skewed to make his point about the importance of infant attachment, so it's instructive to note that recent studies with infants reared in Romanian orphanages confirm his work.

Infants were given minimal custodial care: they were confined to cots, fed with propped-up bottles, having almost no interactions with adult caregivers. These infants were rarely picked up, never hugged or smiled at. Researchers found that the babies' psychological deprivation affected their brain development and resulted in compromises in stress hormone regulation as well as other consequences. (Zigler, Finn-Stevenson, and Hall 2002, 26)

Further research has shown that severely impaired children who were adopted before age two made immense developmental and physical progress by age four, particularly if they were adopted as infants. Thus we are beginning to learn more about the resilience of young children's brains and bodies when positive attachment and interactions are present, as well as about the brain's plasticity and ability to regenerate.

Brain Development through Play, Peer Interaction, and Language Development

In our early childhood settings, we have the means to foster learning not only through individual nurturance, but also by providing specific opportunities for imaginative play and the associated benefits of social interaction and language development. It is now clear that the interactions and opportunities for exploration that play provides are essential for healthy brain development. The importance of play—and play's connection to learning—has been endorsed repeatedly by eminent pediatricians and psychologists, by major groups of early childhood educators such as the Alliance for Childhood, and by the American Academy of Pediatrics.

Dramatic or imaginative play is one of the child's primary avenues for learning. At age two, children are beginning to move from a stage called "parallel play," in which they explore materials side by side but as individuals, to an interactive and imaginative play mode where they play together. Teachers of early childhood development have respect for dramatic play because it requires children to symbolize and use language in a social context. Children who pretend are engaging in symbolic play. Perhaps the child playing "doctor" uses a crayon as a "shot," the "daddy" is cooking inch-cube "meatballs" and stirring some shoelaces in a pot for "spaghetti," and the "dog" curls up on a round pillow "dog bed" in the library corner. All of these play scenarios have implications for symbolic thinking that translate to academic skill development. It follows that to be able to read, a child must understand that written words, those black clumps on a page, have meaning. The child needs to grasp that the black clumps are symbols for spoken words, and eventually that separate letters of the alphabet make up the black clumps. These black clumps are written symbols that stand for the words we speak, just as the crayon is the symbol for a "shot" or hypodermic needle. Mathematically, the child needs to internalize the understanding that a spoken or written number has many other meanings. For instance, the number five can be understood in different ways:

- "Five" is a word in a series of words—"one, two, three, four, five . . ."

- "5" is a mark that looks sort of like an "S."

- "Five" is a concept for a quantity of something, such as five cats, five balls, or five spoons.

When children engage in dramatic play, complex, abstract ideas such as the number five are supported.

The acts of pretending, symbolizing, and putting ideas into words expand the child's thinking, extend language learning, and encourage the creation of narratives and stories that transfer into future imaginative thinking and creative writing. Finally, because it is natural for the child, play is usually characterized by a kind of joyful engagement, a need to persist. This persistence eventually translates into the best kind of practice: meaningful practice at skills that may not be so much fun but are important to master, a kind of disposition to "keep at it until I get it!"

The developing brain is best nurtured by consistent, caring adults; by opportunities to engage with materials and with other children in problem-solving and dramatic-play situations; and by supportive social environments that are positive and pleasurable. This stands in opposition to the training of young children in response to directions and questions. Therefore, the following section of this chapter describes developmental interaction, a recognized and flexible approach to early childhood education that is firmly based in the observation of children and the importance of their interactions—an approach that holds true to core values of growth and development even as it adjusts to changing families and societal challenges.

Plan to attend a professional lecture or conference session on new discoveries in brain development research. Keep notes and handouts to share as you discuss implications for practice with colleagues.

Purchase or rent a video, such as *Scientific American Frontiers: Pieces of Mind* (PBS Home Video 1997), that reviews and explores the developing brain in this exploding area of scientific discovery. Watch the video together as a faculty, and create a plan for showing it to parents at a school community meeting.

Choose a book about the developing brain, such as Rima Shore's *Rethinking the Brain: New Insights into Early Development* (1997) or the Committee on Integrating the Science of Early Childhood Development's *From Neurons to Neighborhoods: The Science of Early Childhood Development* (2000), and select chapters to read and discuss at staff meetings. Make a list of the most important facts that relate to young children's learning, and work together on developing a pamphlet for parents using these facts as a resource.

The Developmental-Interaction Approach

Educational theories may come and go in popularity or change their terminology, but the developmental-interaction approach has maintained its core values over the years. While the values are firm, the approach is not rigid. This helps us avoid the intrinsic danger of observing children's actions for proof of what we *think* we know, instead of looking for insights that children provide us through their play and their interactions.

For example, if we theorize that children's behavior is identical to children's learning, then we might feel that conditioning young children to repeat can and should be seen as a valuable trained behavior. This approach to early childhood education has been most glaringly used in experiments involving the use of flash cards with infants and toddlers in the mistaken belief that regurgitating sounds and words is the same as reading. The reality is that in the warmth of a parent's lap, "success" may be claimed, but it in no way connects to the kinds of early reading behaviors that carry meaning and persist over time. Similarly, in a classroom where the teacher is asking for a single right answer by having three- and four-year-olds repeat "three plus three equals six" from memory, children are not seen as individuals with unique approaches and capabilities. Nor are they treated as individuals at a particular stage of life when learning is closely connected to the senses and to meaningful action. In a mind frame that regards training as identical to teaching, nurture has no place, and meaningful learning is doomed.

In contrast to the examples of repetition described above, the developmental-interaction approach to early childhood education combines wisdom drawn from developmental theories with the understanding that knowledge of individual children informs practice on a day-to-day basis.

Understanding the Ideas Behind the Developmental-Interaction Approach

Developmental psychologists Barbara Biber and Margery B. Franklin explain the theoretical bases of developmental interaction as utilizing two major expressions of the developmental sequence: cognitive-developmental theory, drawing on the work of Heinz Werner and Jean Piaget, and Erik Erikson's ego psychology framework (Biber 1984). They describe cognitive development as "the maturation of the child . . . seen as a series of changing ways of gaining and organizing his knowledge of the universe of things, people, and ideas. In general terms the world he first knows through his senses and his physical-motor maneuvers is fundamentally altered when he can deal symbolically, through verbal and nonverbal modes, with his experience" (287). Describing ego psychology they write, "the stepping stones to healthy personality development spanning the preschool years have been defined as: a sense of trustfulness in others and trustworthiness in one's self; a sense of autonomy through making choices and exercising control; a sense of initiative expressed in a variety of making, doing, and playing activities in cooperation with others" (288). Jean Piaget and Bärbel Inhelder in their definitive summary of Piaget's work also acknowledge the relationship of the affective to the cognitive:

There is no behavior pattern, however intellectual, which does not involve affective factors as motives. . . . Behavior is therefore of a piece, even if the structures do not explain its energetics and if, vice versa, its energetics do not account for its structures. The two aspects, affective and cognitive, are at the same time inseparable and irreducible. (Piaget and Inhelder 1969, 158)

Interpreting the Philosophy

As director of an early childhood center based on developmental inter-action, I found myself frequently challenged by parents to explain the school's philosophy. Their questions often stemmed from personal child-hood memories that involved the direct teaching of letters and numbers. In contrast, our walls, awash in children's artwork, and our classrooms, liber-ally provisioned with blocks and dress-ups, seemed to make them nervous. Where was the alphabet strip of upper- and lowercase letters that should be mounted at the top of a chalkboard (above the heads of children)?

"Well," I'd reply, "the term 'developmental-interaction' may sound a bit fancy, but in truth it's a fascinating philosophy and teaching practice de-voted to your child's *real* learning." I would then make the following two points, always leaving room for parents to interrupt and question.

First, think of development like this: Young children are developing from the moment they are born, developing in every way—physically, emotion-ally, socially, and yes, intellectually. Picture an eighteen-month-old as she drops a toy or a bit of food over the side of her high chair again and again. This is not simple repetition. She is demonstrating

- small motor development and hand-eye coordination

- initiative

- playfulness in the game involving her parent or caregiver

- curiosity concerning cause and effect as each item falls down (rather than up) at a different speed depending on its physical properties

Children develop with different "timetables," temperaments, and rhythms. For instance, your Johnny is crawling and just beginning to pull himself up on the edge of the sofa while your neighbor's child is already walking at nine months. Mouthing and babbling in response to your coos have led to Maria's first words at just over one year, while your best friend's child at age two has a limited vocabulary of "mama," "dada," and "bye-bye." Your quietly observant three-year-old daughter appears overly cautious, and you're wondering if your sister's whirlwind child of the same age is going to have an advantage as an adult. Your four-year-old son has started to recognize words in the books you read to him, but kindergartener Anisa's mother says Anisa seems content to be read to or just look at picture books on her own. All of these differences fall within normal range, and they reflect personal characteristics, family background and style, as well as variable rates of unfolding competencies.

Second, think of interaction in the following ways: Although specific theorists have studied separate areas of development, constant interaction occurs among and between physical-, social-, emotional-, and intellectual-development pathways. A powerful example I like to use is the true story of "Yuki," a Japanese infant who was born with large areas of his brain apparently missing on the pictures of his CAT scan. He could not see or hear, and the prognosis was that he would never walk or develop at all. Because of his mother's constant stimulation of his limbs and all his other senses and the center for neurologically impaired children, where he received daily opportunities for engagement and response, by age four Yuki was able to see, hear, walk, run, smile, and respond to others. Early interaction with others on many levels allowed for the generation of centrally important areas of his brain and its interactive capacities. While this is a dramatic example, less dramatic but equally important examples are observed regularly in early childhood settings: an extremely active child, who has a hard time sitting in a group, may feel so relaxed and good about herself after riding a trike or throwing a ball on the playground that she is able to sit still and listen quietly at story time.

Interaction in the developmental-interaction approach also refers to children's interactions with the environments and the people in their lives. Thus, carefully organized and richly provisioned classrooms provide opportunities for children to engage with materials and to interact with one another in the process. Warm and nurturing teachers facilitate these interactions, providing additional opportunities for children to make discoveries and form appropriate relationships with peers and adults outside their homes.

The graduate faculty at the Bank Street College of Education (where the theory and practice of developmental interaction was developed during decades of research) continue to incorporate current challenges and new thinking into their work. They recognize that adapting developmental interaction to meet today's challenges is an ongoing task related to dramatic changes in society over the course of the twentieth century and continuing into the twenty-first century. These changes include a range of family configurations such as

- households where both parents work outside the home

- single parents struggling to raise children alone, "making do" or in poverty

- households where the mother works outside the home and the father is the full-time caregiver

- lesbian- and gay-headed families

- increasing numbers of families from diverse ethnic and linguistic backgrounds

It follows that these changes mandate the consideration of a variety of challenges, familial, societal, and cultural.

PROFESSIONAL DEVELOPMENT SUGGESTIONS

Plan for each staff member to review your school's or center's philosophy and compare it with the developmental-interaction approach. In a faculty discussion, consider the following questions: Are there common themes and practices? Are there significant differences? Are there aspects of the approach that you might like to adopt?

Plan individual staff visits to a school that espouses the developmental-interaction philosophy. Make written observations. Even if you are already using this approach, you are bound to be stimulated by variations in classroom practice as you share observations at a faculty meeting.

Give staff sufficient time to read *Young Geographers: How They Explore the World and How They Map the World* by Lucy Sprague Mitchell (1991), the founder of Bank Street College of Education, and Sam Brian. Discuss possibilities for integrating some of her ideas into your curriculum.

Chapter 2

Family, Societal, and Cultural Issues

It is said that the only constant is change. Change does not have to compete with theories of how young children grow, develop, and learn. Change does mean, however, that early childhood professionals must be increasingly open to unfamiliar ways of thinking and being. So, along with staying abreast of new realities and possibilities, early childhood educators must adapt to changes in the families they work with. As children from a wide range of backgrounds enter their early childhood programs, educators must be compassionate as they encounter the varying values and customs of children and families.

Changing Families

Two-Parent Families

Two-parent working families from all economic classes generally spend less time with their children than did the traditional two-parent families of the past. With the exception of the most fortunate situations, there is also apt to be less continuity of care in the home. And although many grandparents still play important roles in children's lives, extended family support has become rare.

Given long workdays, parents often must piece together care from sitters, early childhood centers, family child care homes, and after-school programs. One family of modest means hired their unemployed twenty-year-old nephew to look after their three small children, including an infant. With no real interest in the job, the nephew was unable to control the older children, losing his temper and struggling to run the household. All parties expressed frustration and dissatisfaction with the arrangement. Yet for the parents, it was better than their local day care center, and the young man needed the work. For the children, it was a chaotic situation.

In households where a mother works outside the home and consistent care is provided by a father, children benefit from the continuity Dad provides. Care may take place in the home or in combination with center care. Whatever the arrangement, the child can count on seeing the same loving face for a significant time each day. The mother's role is equally important, although time spent with each parent is balanced differently than it was in the 1950s. Teachers and program directors have the task of including fathers in program activities, as well as making sure that mothers are respected in their role as breadwinners—regularly informed and, if possible, present at parent-teacher conferences.

Families headed by gay and lesbian parents with young children are increasingly familiar members of early childhood communities. Research has shown that children from families headed by same-sex parents receive the same loving attention and thoughtful upbringing as children who come from traditional families. These children are comfortable and often proud when talking about their "two mommies" or "two daddies." Children with same-sex parents are fully positioned to grow into high-functioning, open-minded, and caring adults. Given the support of inclusive child care environments and teachers who are openly accepting of their family composition, children in families with gay or lesbian parents demonstrate the same joy and enthusiasm natural to all young children.

Single-Parent Families

As we approach the beginning of the second decade of the twenty-first century, the national divorce rate continues to increase. This does not mean that children of divorced families are unloved or uncared for. Nevertheless, many children must adjust to living in two different households, the amount of time determined by a specific divorce settlement. These children may live part-time in two households, which may be single-parent, two-parent, or blended families with children from previous marriages. Children may also experience the arrival of new siblings in separate households. Situations such as these require a significant effort on the part of children to adjust and readjust to the rhythms of different households. Teacher-caregivers need to be alert and sensitive to changes in behavior or fatigue when the changeover from one home to another occurs. Early childhood educators can give invaluable support by providing time for children to express their feelings, rest, or just take a break. If a worrisome pattern emerges, the school, center, or child care program can work with the parents to minimize stress.

Some children may live with a mother or father who has been abandoned by the other parent. This situation carries added stressors for the child, whose primary parent may become depressed or disorganized in the struggle to keep herself or himself together, to hold down a job, and to find child care.

Single parenting can also be elective. In this scenario, the parent will usually have thought the process through and put support systems in place. In any case, single parents need considerable support from directors and teachers of early childhood programs. The children themselves require assurance that the adults in their lives are working together closely, thus providing a sense of stability that lies at the root of nurturance.

Families and Children Placed at Risk by Poverty

Poverty can affect two-parent as well as single-parent families, adding a host of additional stressors. Living arrangements are cramped, providing little space to allow for young children's adequate sleeping arrangements and their need to move about. Besides worrying about money for food and rent, poor families often have to cope with untenable and often dangerous situations that may include unsanitary living conditions, peeling paint, erratic heat and water supplies, and unsafe building maintenance. In the severest circumstances, parents and children are forced to live in temporary homeless shelters—from which they may be moved at any moment—accompanied by the associated confusion of changing schools.

Poor, single parents and their children are particularly vulnerable, even when the parent manages to hold a job and make ends meet. For instance, a single mother may find reasonable child care arrangements and secure a job, but this may push her income higher, to a level where she will be denied welfare payments or food stamps. In this situation, something has to give, and it may well be the job and the child care arrangement that the mother now cannot afford.

Even with the best of intentions, families struggling in poverty may be unable to provide their children with the stability and responsiveness essential for healthy growth and development. Early childhood teachers who provide responsive care for infants and young children in poverty must also gain parental trust and overcome feelings of embarrassment related to the circumstances of poverty. Teachers working with this vulnerable population have to keep children's resilience and their natural disposition to learn and explore in the forefront. At the same time, teachers must take into account possibilities that may include inadequate food and limited access to health care. For the children, coming to a familiar child care setting each day can create a sense of safety and security that may be lacking in their home environments. Directors of early childhood programs play an important role by working closely with teachers to support children's bodily as well as emotional nourishment and to help parents with practical advice in seeking social services.

Cultural Differences

Teaching young children today demands a willingness to understand unfamiliar points of view, a variety of customs, and different conditions of living. To do this, we have to understand the way we ourselves think and act on a cultural level. Developmentally appropriate teachers face the challenge of knowing that the goals of human development vary considerably according to the cultural traditions and circumstances of different communities (Rogoff 2003). To put this in perspective, let's look for an extreme example in a country that is far away from our own. Infants in Bali are restrained from crawling based on religious beliefs of the culture, combined with pragmatic cautions because of the dirt floors of Balinese homes, yet they learn to walk as competently as children in other parts of the world.

Educators in early childhood settings throughout the United States and Canada encounter a wide range of differences among the children and families they work with. Cynthia Ballenger's (1999) experiences teaching "other people's children" of Haitian background in a bilingual threes class are eye-opening as she comes to recognize her own Westernized attitudes toward books and literacy learning in contrast to the children's strong oral tradition. Honestly examining her own teaching practice with colleagues helps Cynthia to see the children's literacy strengths as they strive to make connections with printed letters and words. She also learns important lessons about Haitian parents' expectations and ways of responding to their children's behaviors that initially clash with her own views of discipline.

Considerable consensus is found among experts in the field of cultural diversity and early childhood education concerning teacher attitudes as they encounter an increasing number of children from varied backgrounds (Bowman and Moore 2006). Children who feel accepted by their teachers will come to trust them. Teacher-caregivers need to be aware of cultural differences and able to use these differences to motivate learning, while at the same time see each child as a unique person. This is a tall order, but some basic premises may serve as useful guidelines in looking at

- cultural differences in communication

- the special challenges of working with children for whom English is a second language

- specific issues related to our work with Latino and African American families whose children represent the largest non-majority cultures in our classrooms

Basic Guidelines for Noticing Cultural Differences in Communication

As a part of mainstream Western culture, early childhood educators in the United States and Canada rely primarily on verbal communication that is usually linear in nature. For instance, when we are reading a story aloud to a group of children, we expect them to learn to look at the pictures and listen to the text. As experienced educators, we expect the youngest children to insert non sequiturs such as "Do you know I'm going to go home with Juan after school today?!" But we are less prepared for older children jumping in with their personal "takes" and additions that are seemingly irrelevant. For culturally sensitive teachers, the questions that then arise may relate to the children's previous experience with text, and whether their primary connection with story is one of oral tradition and storytelling rather than print.

In Native American, South American, and Asian cultures (to name only a few), accepted or "normal" ways of conveying meaning can be more varied. Cultures differ in many ways. For example

- condoning the use of eye contact, which may only be acceptable in certain situations

- sanctioning appropriate times to talk, or not to talk

- encouraging or discouraging specific body language

- expressing anger in various ways

As we become more aware of these differences in children's behavior and adjust our expectations, we examine our own manner of expression. For instance, our early childhood teaching practices support the role of teachers as gentle and inquiring, often using language such as "Would you like to . . . ?" or "I need you to stop doing (or do) what I asked." We tend to alter our tone of voice to indicate when we "mean business." This invitational style or indirect approach to guidance and discipline may not fit with either language or expectations in some children's homes.

Getting to know the families in our school communities is crucial to finding approaches that maintain our integrity as teachers while at the same time incorporate techniques familiar to the children we serve.

Working with Children for Whom English Is a Second Language

As young children learn to speak a native language at home, they are also learning to think. Parents who are English-language speakers are constantly amazed at their children's growing vocabularies and progressive ability to express thoughts and feelings. The same is true of families who speak another language at home. Nevertheless, non–English-speaking children who enter a child care program, school, or other early childhood setting in the United States face a disconcerting situation: the language of the classroom is not the language they understand. Although it is important for non–English-speaking children to learn English, it must not be forced at the expense of giving up the language in which they learned to communicate and comprehend. Language is also closely connected to culture. It is logical, therefore, that unless teacher-caregivers accept the customs and language of non–English-speaking children, we run the risk of interfering with the children's intellectual as well as social development.

In her book *Room for Talk,* Rebekah Fassler (2003) introduces us to a kindergarten teacher's inspiring success in working with a class of multilingual children as she goes about nurturing their social and cognitive development. The teacher, "Mrs. Barker," herself speaks only English. The children in her classroom of thirty-two students are native speakers of Chinese, Russian, Turkish, Vietnamese, Albanian, and Spanish. In describing Mrs. Barker's teaching practices, Fassler demonstrates how a community can be constructed by helping children of multilingual backgrounds make connections with one another through spontaneous, meaningful interactions. In group games Mrs. Barker encourages communication that is at first physical, as one child in the circle rolls or throws a ball to another saying his or her name aloud. She groups children together by interest rather than language and watches as verbal interactions grow and incorporate English words. She reads picture books and teaches songs in English. Her "skills teaching" is conducted in English as a communal affair to which everyone contributes at his or her readiness level.

Working with Latino Families

Latino (or Hispanic) families comprise the fastest growing non-majority culture in the United States. Latino families have specific characteristics depending on their cultural origins, be they Mexican American, Puerto Rican, Central or South American, or from one of the culturally distinct Caribbean islands. Despite these differences, Latino families usually share a common language and, in general, embrace specific values. One of the most central values is the emphasis on family. Respect for others, particularly for adults, is another important Latino value that may manifest itself in the classroom by apparent passivity in group discussion or reluctance to raise one's hand (which might be perceived as challenging the teacher or a fellow classmate). This reticence can be compounded by the deep regard for education and teachers held by Latino families. Early childhood classrooms, where opportunities for choice and informal communication abound, are important for children but may seem antithetical to more formal educational practices associated with traditional Latino views of teaching and learning. Teachers who understand this will not only want to consider general issues related to working with children for whom English is a second language, but also wish to interpret their informal practice to these families. At the same time they will want to consider the possibility of introducing some formal elements—perhaps during group times, games, or songs.

Working with African American Families

Families of African American origin account for, along with Latino families, the largest non-majority culture in the United States. In the past, to quote historian Nell Irvin Painter, "race—as African descent—trumped every other facet of identity: mixed-race people became simply black, and other ancestors simply disappeared. Immigrants of African ancestry, regardless of where they came from or what languages they spoke, became simply black. No matter how rich or poor, no matter where they lived, no matter how well or little educated, African Americans of any class became simply black" (Painter 2006, 337).

Painter's description is more infrequent today. Black and other minority Americans are less often seen as faceless groups lacking individuality. Nevertheless, despite significant contributions to American cultural heritage and the goals of integration and equal opportunity for African American children espoused since the 1960s, we have made minimal progress in improving their lives and educational opportunities. Among others, Jonathan Kozol's books addressing the inequities in our society have served as a collective conscience. We may be able to identify many successful, prominent, and affluent African Americans, yet the probability is that as early childhood educators we will be working with young children who have had little access to enrichment opportunities in the home as a result of poverty and stressful living conditions.

Language development is closely linked to brain development. Frequent opportunities for conversation and vocabulary enrichment are important for all children in early childhood settings, especially for those who have had limited opportunity for discussion at home. African American children may arrive in school using nonstandard English (sometimes called African American vernacular English). It's our job to nurture their efforts at self-expression rather than to correct them. The rhythms and speech patterns of African American vernacular English lend themselves to play with words, rhyme, and song. Let's not forget that rap music is an accepted creative mode of expression. At the same time, it's our job to use and introduce Standard English to African American children in as many natural ways as possible. A mainstream mode of expression will be important as they enter grade school—and in their future lives.

Lisa Delpit (1995) and others have urged teachers to think about their own manners of expression. As in some other cultural contexts, teachers' "inviting" children to participate in activities may be misconstrued as a mere choice. In other words, "If you wanted me to do it, why didn't you just tell me?" In thinking about effective ways to communicate with African American children, teachers may want to consider asking direct questions and contributing information with clear, meaningful intent. They can bypass direct instruction and integrate nonstandard speech patterns with Standard English by creating an experience chart, taking down the children's own words as part of a project, group story, chant, or letter and altering some of the words into Standard English spellings. In this scenario, children read along as the teacher honors their dictation, while simultaneously being exposed to the standard spellings and syntax of the written text. Another tactic is to read aloud a classic folktale, such as "The Three Billy Goats Gruff" or an Anansi spider tale. Because young children are often motivated by folktales to take on roles and act out the plots, it's easy to accept nonstandard English interpretations while they gain practice in reenacting the beginning, middle, and end of a traditional story.

Being open to difference and embracing the unfamiliar are prerequisites for effective teaching and the administration of early childhood programs. Meeting families on their ground and seeking them out no matter how difficult the challenges are basic to becoming effective partners. Children, who understand more about the adults in their lives than we often remember, are very aware of the unity or discord of adult support. Despite their resilience, we owe children partnerships between home and school that nourish confidence and joy.

PROFESSIONAL DEVELOPMENT SUGGESTIONS

Read a work from the professional literature that deals with issues of diversity, and discuss it at a staff meeting. You may wish to use one of the works cited in this chapter (a list of references can be found beginning on page 135). Vivian Paley (2000) gives us her personal reflections on race and on being a white teacher in an interracial kindergarten classroom; Virginia Casper and Steven Schultz (1999) help us to explore working with lesbian- and gay-headed families as they confront our homophobia; Rebekah Fassler (2003) and Cynthia Ballenger (1999) bring cultural and linguistic perspectives to our thinking; Nell Irvin Painter (2006) creates a historical perspective on the African American experience in our country. As you read, focus on your personal feelings and how the author may have affected your thinking. Prepare for an honest and civil sharing of opinions.

Identify a current societal challenge that you would like to know more about, and choose a professional book, such as Valerie Polakow's *Lives on the Edge: Single Mothers and Their Children in the Other America* (1993), to explore issues of race, class, ethnicity, or family configuration. Make a list that breaks down the information into categories such as "Something I Knew," "Something I Learned," "Something I Questioned." Discuss the book and its issues with colleagues at a formal or informal staff gathering.

Attend a professional conference of early childhood educators of a different ethnic or cultural background from yours. This takes courage, and it is an experience that one or two staff members may share with the whole faculty on their return. As you question yourself, keep a journal of your feelings and interactions: Will you be accepted by workshop participants whose backgrounds are unlike your own? Will you yourself be open enough to accept and respect adults who don't share your point of view? In addition to the professional development opportunities offered, this experience can reinforce the confidence that despite differences of opinion and experience, you will learn how much you have in common with fellow human beings of markedly diverse backgrounds and beliefs.

Chapter 3

Multiple Intelligences Theory

I was a graduate student in 1983 when Howard Gardner's *Frames of Mind* was first published. One of my teachers assigned a new book to each member of our seminar, and it was my luck to be handed Dr. Gardner's huge and seemingly dense volume to report on to the rest of the class. I knew that Howard Gardner was a professor of developmental theory and neuropsychology, but nothing prepared me for the power of his idea that intelligence could be viewed from the perspective of individual children's strengths.

Over the years, Dr. Gardner has refined and expanded his theory, but his initial premise has never changed: an individual's unique strengths cannot be determined by a single assessment, such as an IQ test, that relies heavily on quantifiable verbal and mathematical measurements. A specific image from the television screen that stayed with me during my first exposure to multiple intelligences (MI) theory was football quarterback Joe Montana throwing and catching a football with breathtaking precision time after time. What kind of uncanny estimation did his mind-body connection—his bodily-kinesthetic intelligence—calculate to achieve these feats of perfection? Another thought came as I contemplated Gardner's concepts of interpersonal and intrapersonal intelligence. Weren't these skills of communication and self-knowledge identical to the interactions and reflections good teachers demonstrate in their work with children and families?

And what about the possible influence of multiple intelligences theory on parents? Would thinking about their children's individual gifts, their innate dispositions, encourage parents to acknowledge unique competencies, resulting in their children's increased confidence and self-esteem in all areas of learning?

Howard Gardner gives us a personal glimpse into his thinking about the origins of multiple intelligences theory, helping us connect it to developmental theories. He writes:

> When I was a youth, music in particular and the arts in general were important parts of my life. Therefore, when I began to think of what it meant to be "developed," when I asked myself what optimal human development is, I became convinced that developmentalists had to pay much more attention to the skills and capacities of painters, writers, musicians, dancers, and other artists. Stimulated (rather than intimidated) by the prospect of broadening the definition of *cognition,* I found it comfortable to deem the capacities of those in the arts as fully cognitive—no less cognitive than skills of mathematicians and scientists, as viewed by my fellow developmental psychologists. (Gardner 1999, 28)

Gardner is very clear in asserting that "all of us have the full range of intelligences; that is what makes us human beings, cognitively speaking," but that "no two individuals—not even identical twins—have exactly the same intellectual profile because, even when the genetic material is identical, individuals have different experiences" (Gardner 2006, 23).

Gardner defines an intelligence as

> a capacity to process a certain kind of information—that originates in human biology and human psychology. . . . An intelligence entails the ability to solve problems or fashion products that are of consequence in a particular cultural setting or community. . . . MI theory is framed in light of the biological origins of each problem-solving skill. . . . Even so, the biological proclivity to participate in a particular form of problem solving must also be coupled with the cultural nurturing of that domain. For example, language, a universal skill, may manifest itself particularly as writing in one culture, as oratory in another culture, and as the secret language composed of anagrams or tongue twisters in a third. (Gardner 2006, 6–7)

The seven original intelligences identified by Gardner do not operate in isolation and are not ordered according to their importance, although the first two have particular prominence in schools:

- linguistic intelligence
- logical-mathematical intelligence
- musical intelligence
- bodily-kinesthetic intelligence
- spatial intelligence
- interpersonal intelligence
- intrapersonal intelligence

Gardner has identified two additional intelligences that may be added to the original list:

- naturalist intelligence
- existential intelligence or the "intelligence of big questions"

The following sections present a discussion of Gardner's intelligences. To illustrate each intelligence, I have chosen to share a short story about one or more individuals from a variety of backgrounds who demonstrated some specific dispositions—intelligences—in childhood that led to later success. For each intelligence, I provide a vignette (In the Classroom) of a child whom you might teach in your own early childhood classroom.

Linguistic Intelligence

Linguistic intelligence "involves sensitivity to spoken and written language, the ability to learn languages, and the capacity to use language to accomplish certain goals" (Gardner 1999, 41).

In the early 1800s, four Brontë children—Charlotte, Branwell, Emily, and Anne—were born within the space of five years and went on to survive two elder sisters who died from tuberculosis. Though small in size, their home was surrounded by the vast Yorkshire moors of England. Until their mother died a year after Anne's birth, they enjoyed an informal family life. Perhaps because of their loss and the isolated nature of their existence, the children reveled in making up stories. They read the romantic novels of Sir Walter Scott and the poems of Wordsworth and Byron. Creating imaginary worlds and writing about them became a passion. Charlotte and brother Branwell, who had been given a set of wooden soldiers by his father, created the kingdom of Angria (perhaps based on Swift's *Gulliver's Travels*), which they wrote about in tiny notebooks. Emily and Anne made up their own epic about the kingdom of Gondal. And although Branwell did not continue to write, we are grateful for the imaginative literary play of these children that later produced masterworks exemplified by Charlotte's *Jane Eyre* and Emily's *Wuthering Heights*.

A century after the Brontës, another famous author-to-be was born far from England in Lorain, Ohio. As a child, Chloe was a voracious reader of a wide range of authors. Her special favorites were Leo Tolstoy and Jane Austen. Her father was a ship welder and master storyteller, and it was from him that Chloe heard her first African American folktales. In the early 1950s Chloe went to college at Howard University, where she became known as Toni. A fellow undergraduate student at Howard University remembers the excitement when word got around that Toni was going to tell a story. These few brief facts give us a glimpse into the early manifestations of the linguistic genius of Toni Morrison, who gave us *The Bluest Eye* and the Pulitzer Prize–winning *Beloved*. Morrison has written about herself: "Writing never made me happy. Writing never made me suffer. I have had misfortunes small and large, yet all through them nothing could keep me from doing it. And nothing could satiate my appetite for others who did" (Morrison 1997, 14).

In the Classroom

This year you have two children in your fours class who stand out in terms of their affinity for language, though both demonstrate this in unique ways. Christine is perfunctory in her verbal interactions but is fascinated by all aspects of the written word. Jimmy, on the other hand, expresses himself with sophisticated language and is already a reader, requesting that you find him chapter books, especially "the one about the wizard of Oz!" Both children are avid listeners at story time.

Your room is richly provisioned with materials for experimenting with writing, an inviting book display, and many activities to inspire conversations. As you watch Christine approach the writing table, you remember that she entered class in September already able to write her name with a secure hand, letters evenly spaced and well formed. Now, midway through the year, she has begun to experiment with inventive spelling and is starting to write short two-line stories. You have done some group work with phonics and phonemic awareness, focusing on words that hold the most interest for the class (their names, favorite rhymes and songs). You notice that Christine appears to have incorporated a wealth of additional information about the relationship between sounds and letters on her own, using her knowledge to communicate with others through stories, cards, and brief letters to Grandma.

Jimmy, however, couldn't care less about writing. In fact his distaste for putting crayon or pencil to paper is only matched by Christine's resistance to reading. He is happiest when engaged in a lively conversation with another child or deeply concentrating on a book he has chosen to read. He has graduated from "I Can Read" books to those with content that particularly interests him.

Both Christine and Jimmy are deeply absorbed when engaged in language activities that appeal to them. Your hunch is that by nurturing these individual interests and abilities—while continuing to engage them in a range of activities—their linguistic intelligence will eventually expand into fluid use of the interconnected skills of reading, writing, listening, and speaking.

Logical-Mathematical Intelligence

Logical-mathematical intelligence "involves the capacity to analyze problems logically, carry out mathematical operations, and investigate issues scientifically" (Gardner 1999, 42).

It's fascinating (and instructive in light of mainstream emphasis on linguistic intelligence) to learn that Albert Einstein's parents were worried about his intellectual development because of a language delay and his inability to speak fluently until he was nine years old. An early personal memory concerning a pocket compass shown to him by his father at age five allows us to take a peek into his mind. The compass was a revelation, giving Albert the sense that an element of "empty space" was in some way making the compass needle move. As a young child, though linguistically challenged, Einstein was good at math, models, and things mechanical. He did well in elementary school. At ten, a family friend introduced him to scientific and philosophical writings, and at twelve he taught himself Euclidean geometry. Einstein always felt that the ability to learn on his own was more important than any top-down teaching could ever be.

In 1875 (four years before Albert Einstein was born), five-year-old Maria Montessori moved from the small town of Ancona, Italy, to Rome. She began the study of engineering when she was thirteen with the support of both her father and her mother. It was quite an accomplishment when later she was accepted as a medical student to the University of Rome and graduated as Italy's first female doctor. Montessori's background as a physician, her intense interest in children, and her work with the mentally challenged set the stage for her carefully considered view of education. Using a scientific lens, combined with her vibrant imagination, she created materials and an educational program that were based on astute observations of young children, their needs, and the particular social contexts of the time in which she lived. The Montessori method is still an influential force in early childhood education.

In the Classroom

Five-year-old Radu is new to your mixed-age classroom of threes, fours, and fives and equally new to the United States. Both of his parents were practicing engineers in their native Romania, and they have told the school's director that Radu is a mathematical genius. Other teachers at your school seemed wary of the idea of accepting this little boy into their classrooms, perhaps intimidated by the parents' pronouncement and their own mathematical limitations. You, however, decided to accept the challenge. Radu is, after all, a five-year-old child with similarities to other five-year-olds as well as unique differences.

Radu speaks limited English but appears to understand the other children in your class. Tall and bespectacled, he seems drawn to the younger children, with whom he shows a playful and boisterous side. The one-on-one correspondence activities engaged in enthusiastically by the rest of the class, such as matching cups to napkins at snack time, hold no interest for him whatsoever. When counting numbers of children who are present during morning attendance, Radu snaps with some irritation, "Four not here!" Paper and pencil are his friends. He will work on a delicate symmetrical drawing for long periods of time or contentedly create strings of algorithms.

As parent-teacher conferences approach, you face a dilemma. You are certainly not equipped to further Radu's prodigious mathematical skills, but you are aware that it's important to acknowledge them. You also know it is vital to encourage appropriate interaction between Radu and the older children in the class. You decide to tell his parents that you are going to honor Radu's abilities by encouraging him to translate his skill with numbers and proportion to the unit block area, where he will also have more contact with children closer to his age. Nurturing other aspects of Radu's development can only strengthen him as a developing child while supporting his unique logical-mathematical gifts.

Musical Intelligence

Musical intelligence "entails skill in the performance, composition, and appreciation of musical patterns" (Gardner 1999, 42).

In the 1920s the di Bonaventura family, recent immigrants from Italy, settled in a small town in West Virginia to make a new life and to raise their children. Sabbatino, the eldest, seemed to love music, so when he was six years old, his parents took him to see the local music teacher, who started him on the violin; soon he was playing with obvious musicality and excellent technique. After Sabbatino came Anna and then Mario, two more violin prodigies. Four years later Antonio arrived. The family needed a pianist, and Antonio obliged with the same musical sensibilities as his siblings.

After the children played together on local movie theater stages, their teacher told their parents that the family had to relocate to New York City. She no longer knew enough to help them progress. And so, much sacrifice and many scholarships later, Sabbatino ("Dr. Sam") went on to become a beloved professor of violin and composition at a well-known music conservatory. Anna spent many years as a choral conductor. Mario became a gifted composer, conductor, and champion of contemporary music. Anthony is an internationally acclaimed concert pianist. Where did this talent come from? No one in the family knows. What we do know is that these children displayed musical intelligence at an early age, and that their talents were recognized, encouraged, and nurtured by their family and their teachers.

In the Classroom

Three-year-old Sheila is having a resurgence of separation anxiety. You've tried a number of different tactics to ease her into the room, including meeting Sheila and her mother at the school door, bringing one of her special friends with you, and talking about a new collage project you feel she will be drawn to.

Sheila's family is of Irish descent, and you suddenly remember the CD of Irish folk music the family brought in at the beginning of the year. You put on the music before Sheila arrives, and soon after entering the classroom, her crying stops, and she begins to dance! Sheila's eyes light up, and other children join in with their own versions of the folk dance. This is the moment when you begin to look at Sheila through a rhythmic and musical lens. You realize that all year, music time has been one of her favorite parts of the day. You notice how fluidly her body moves, and the way her feet reflect the rhythm of the music—even though her dance is free form rather than learned choreography. You also note the glow reflected on her face and the way other children naturally surround her.

Sheila is a child with a strong feeling for music, and this is a strength you will want to share with her family at the next parent-teacher conference. You, as her teacher, will experiment with different kinds of musical experiences in the classroom. Does this mean that music (and movement) will be a major force in Sheila's life? You can't know for sure, but you do know that you have recognized this child's musical intelligence and will nurture it to the best of your ability.

Bodily-Kinesthetic Intelligence

Bodily-kinesthetic intelligence "entails the potential of using one's whole body or parts of the body (like the hand or the mouth) to solve problems or fashion products" (Gardner 1999, 42).

He was born on a train crossing Siberia to the area known as Soviet Bashkiria. His amazing talent was noticed first as a child dancer in folk performances, but because of World War II, he was unable to join a major ballet school until his middle teens. His fiery temperament brought passion to his art, but this same temperament got him into trouble with the Soviet authorities, who kept him from traveling abroad. After he defected to the West in the 1960s, Rudolf Nureyev's fame spread throughout the world. A magnificent example of bodily-kinesthetic intelligence, he also illustrates the fusing of two intelligences—the musical and the physical. For those fortunate enough to have seen him dance, his ability to be airborne and to land with musical perfection and abandon is an experience never to be forgotten.

In a sport that uses the body and the mind in a very different way, Michelle Wie has achieved amazing triumphs even as a teenager. This young Korean American golfer began learning her sport at age four and at age eleven shot a score of sixty-four for eighteen holes—a feat that many adult male golfers would be thrilled to achieve. Her impressive record and forays as a professional into men's tournaments make it hard to believe that she has only just reached college age.

In the Classroom

Michael is a petite four-year-old with a wiry body, thin arms, and spindly-looking legs. He's constantly on the move. In fact, in your classroom he's a handful when it comes to getting involved and staying with a particular material or project. Group times are especially difficult, as Michael tries a spontaneous cartwheel during read-aloud, pokes or pats other children, or begins to crawl around the edge of the circle. The twinkle in his eye indicates a mischievous nature, rather than a sense that he's out of control. On the playground, however, Michael is extremely focused no matter what activity he's chosen. Peddling a tricycle with expert skill, he moves with speed and care along the trike paths. He is possessed of an active imagination; other children gravitate to him as he organizes a game based on a currently popular children's adventure film. Alone with a soccer ball, he is able to maneuver the ball with ease—though occasionally collapsing in a tangle of arms and legs after executing a particularly strong kick. This is one well-coordinated child! You've noticed that when meeting time occurs after an outdoor play period, Michael seems more relaxed.

You decide to highlight Michael's excellent physical coordination at your next scheduled parent-teacher conference. Michael's parents are concerned about what they perceive as his lack of focus. Brainstorming avenues for physical release may help you all to see his active nature as an important strength. Later on, a specific sports program may be a good choice, but right now you are thinking about engaging Michael with a few other children in a ball game that involves throwing and catching as well as kicking. Block building may be a better source of focus in the classroom than smaller manipulatives and tabletop activities at this time, although you will continue to offer and suggest a range of classroom opportunities as you consciously acknowledge and nurture Michael's bodily-kinesthetic intelligence.

Spatial Intelligence

Spatial intelligence "features the potential to recognize and manipulate the patterns of wide space as well as patterns of more confined areas" (Gardner 1999, 42).

A true story that I love about the great modern architect Frank Lloyd Wright's childhood is intimately connected with educational materials. His mother gave the young Frank a set of geometric blocks designed by Friedrich Froebel as kindergarten "gifts." Later Wright remembered,

Taken East at the age of three to my father's pastorate near Boston, for several years I sat at the little kindergarten table-top ruled by lines about four inches apart each way making four-inch squares; and among other things, played upon these "unit-lines" with the square (cube), the circle (sphere) and the triangle (tetrahedron or tripod)—these were smooth maple-wood blocks. Scarlet cardboard triangles (60°-30°), two inches on the short side, and one side white, were smooth triangular sections with which to come by pattern—design—by my own imagination. Eventually I was to construct designs in other mediums. But the smooth cardboard triangles and maple-wood blocks were most important. All are in my fingers to this day. (Brosterman and Togashi 1997, 138)

Reading his own words, one can almost experience Wright's early discoveries with him and understand their contribution to an innate flair for design that eventually resulted in unique architectural structures.

Spatial thinking can also manifest itself in confined spaces controlled by a strict set of rules. Three Hungarian chess champions, sisters Susan, Sofia, and Judit Polgar, achieved fame in chess tournaments throughout the world as very young players with distinct styles. Their first coach was their father, who emphasized visualization, pattern recognition, and speed. Susan, who began playing in competitions at age four, remembers that the girls played blindfolded-and-blitz chess and practiced solving chess puzzles in early childhood. At age twelve, Judit was classified as one of four supreme chess prodigies in history. Together as children and then as young women, the Polgars put to rest the idea that chess was a man's game by demonstrating the powerful spatial skills that led to their prominence. Today, Susan Polgar (who as a gifted linguist also speaks seven languages) works through her own foundation toward the goal of introducing chess to every child in every school.

In the Classroom

Miguel is a three-year-old bilingual child with an expressive, outgoing nature. He appears to be enthusiastic about every aspect of your program and (inspired by his father's occupation) particularly enjoys taking the role of the chef in the dramatic-play area. Children are drawn to him, so materials that for some might invite solitary activity, such as puzzles or easel painting, automatically turn into avenues for lively conversations, mutual problem solving, and shared creativity. Miguel regularly volunteers information at group meeting times, and enjoys every task on the job chart. He listens intently to stories during read-aloud and takes full advantage of the playground climber and sandbox. His healthy appetite is evident at snack time, though he never takes a leftover cookie without checking first to see if it's "up for grabs." In short, Miguel is a pleasure to have in your classroom

Miguel also loves the block-building area, and one Friday afternoon as you review photographs you've taken of the week's block buildings, you notice several particularly intricate and well-designed structures. They all turn out to be Miguel's creations. The following week you mount several large photographs of buildings and city skylines at the children's eye level near the block area and resolve to observe Miguel's block building process more closely. On Tuesday, you watch as Miguel directs a group of friends in an effort to re-create one of the city skyline scenes. You see him carefully balance a series of unit blocks one atop the other and then stop abruptly. He moves backwards, assessing his work, then moves close to the photograph and touches the top of a specific building in the picture. Off he goes again, this time to find a small half unit and triangle on the block shelf. He returns to his structure and adds the blocks carefully to the top. A huge beam lights up his face as he takes another look at the photograph.

As you reflect on what you've just observed, you realize that you've witnessed not only sophisticated three-year-old block building but also a powerful example of spatial intelligence. Perhaps your next step in nurturing Miguel's skill will be to have him help you select some new block accessories from a catalog or to add that basket of colored inch cubes you've been saving for the classroom block collection.

Interpersonal Intelligence

Interpersonal intelligence "denotes a person's capacity to understand the intentions, motivations, and desires of other people and, consequently, to work effectively with others" (Gardner 1999, 43). Gardner also describes interpersonal intelligence as building "on a core capacity to notice distinctions among others—in particular, contrasts in their moods, temperaments, motivations, and intentions" (Gardner 2006, 15).

Sylvia Ashton-Warner was born in New Zealand in 1905 into a family of nine children. She had a difficult childhood and initially entered teaching to earn a living. Although she demonstrated multiple intelligences as a novelist, pianist, and artist, it is through her unique work with Maori children, and her discovery of the deep connections their own powerful words made for them in the reading and writing process, that her interpersonal intelligence is revealed. Ashton-Warner's remarkable book *Teacher* (1986) shows us the power of what she named the "key vocabulary," stemming from her understanding of the customs and conditions characteristic of the Maori families whose children she taught. Her honesty and empathy in working with aboriginal and mainstream New Zealand children informed her understanding of all children's passions and their need for meaningful expression in the educational process.

Thirty years later in the United States, a young African American boy was growing up in Chicago. James Comer's father worked in a steel mill, and the family's income was helped by his mother's housecleaning and the family's small entrepreneurial projects. The groundwork for Dr. James Comer's major achievements as a child psychiatrist and visionary in the field of school reform was established during his childhood.

> Dinner was the time we were all together. On birthdays and like occasions Mom prepared the favorite dish of each child and managed to make us all feel special. At the dinner table we were expected to talk about school or anything else—ideas, concerns, problems—and we didn't have to be encouraged. . . . Neither Mom nor Dad ever denied the existence of the race problem, but we were not to be victimized by it. My father often said, "Never let your race stop you from doing anything you want to do." (Comer 1997, 24)

Dr. Comer's gifts for communication, nurtured by his parents, resulted in the internationally renowned Comer School Development Program, which fosters connections between schools, families, and communities for the healthy development of all children.

In the Classroom

Five-year-old Nancy was born with cerebral palsy. She has been placed in your mixed-age classroom to expose her to children her own age as well as those who are younger and therefore presumably less mature (threes and fours).

On her first day in your class, Nancy enters with her unsteady gait, legs in braces, her arms waving, and a broad smile on her face. As you kneel down to greet her, she embraces you with a big hug. Nancy is difficult to understand, but this does not keep her from speaking to other children and, if necessary, patiently finding ways to show them what she means. You worry that she may be ignored or rebuffed, but this does not happen. Her big, warm smile seems to light up the room, and her efforts to use many materials are met with success. Dramatic play is her favorite activity, and she often can be found surrounded by a group of younger children caring for their doll babies.

As the weeks go by, it becomes clear that Nancy is also a perceptive and empathic child. When another girl or boy seems distressed or angry, Nancy will drop what she's doing and move directly toward the child for a pat and a "You alright?" She joins in counting and matching games with gusto and spends time with picture books. It's soon evident that she is a beginning reader. Attentive at group times, Nancy joins in singing and even participates in group games like Duck, Duck, Goose. The other children respect and seem to look up to her. As you gather examples of work for your upcoming conference with her parents, you think especially about the role she has played in drawing the class together. Her warmth, enthusiasm, and ever-present interpersonal intelligence are unique personality traits. They also reflect the difficult work Nancy and her parents have done (and continue to do) as they face daily bouts of physical therapy with determination and a positive spirit. You know that your job as Nancy's teacher is to nurture the family's success as you expose Nancy to increasing challenges in your classroom. You will recommend that Nancy attend her fine local public kindergarten in September, confident that her interpersonal strengths will be recognized.

Intrapersonal Intelligence

Intrapersonal intelligence "involves the capacity to understand oneself, to have an effective working model of oneself—including one's own desires, fears, and capacities—and to use such information effectively in regulating one's own life" (Gardner 1999, 43). It implies the ability to use self-understanding to lead a life, both personal and work-related, that is illuminated by the consciousness of one's emotions. Teachers must have at least a degree of this kind of intelligence, as well as interpersonal intelligence, to work with children in balanced and empathic ways.

Sigmund Freud, the founder of psychoanalytic psychology, is a prime example of intrapersonal intelligence. A brilliant child, he entered high school in 1865 at age nine and medical school at the University of Vienna at age seventeen. Dr. Freud's own self-analysis was an intense process of looking inward, exploring his dreams, and examining the early influences that caused the development of his particular personality. This led him to construct groundbreaking theories of the unconscious mind, which he shaped and revised throughout his life in his work with patients and as a gifted writer and professor.

Looking inward for different reasons, a twelve-year-old Macedonian girl named Agnes Gonxha Bojaxhiu believed that God was calling her to be a missionary. In 1928, she joined the Irish Order of the Sisters of Loreto and was sent to India at age eighteen. As a young nun, she worked in Calcutta with its most destitute inhabitants. Agnes, also known as Mother Teresa, was never without an inner vision. Founding the Order of the Missionaries of Charity, her entire life was devoted to helping the ailing and the poor throughout the world. She received the Nobel Peace Prize in 1979.

In the Classroom

David entered your kindergarten–first grade classroom in the fall accompanied by his parents, who were anxious about his fitting in. They chose to give their son a transitional year because of his small stature, his quiet nature, and their concerns about his difficulty in holding and manipulating a pencil. It's true that David's lack of grapho-motor skills gave him trouble in grasping any kind of writing implement, but this is the only area that you could categorize as immature. David is a listener, a watcher, and an interpreter of what's going on around him. Other children like him, but he makes it clear that there are times when he wants to play or work by himself.

Meeting times often illustrate David's range and depth of thinking, reflective of his acute observational skills. For instance, during a discussion of the solar system David comments, "It's a fine idea to talk about our making planets out of papier-mâché and hanging them in the classroom. It could even be fun. But we have to understand that their sizes can only be . . . sort of . . . related to each other the way the real ones are. And we'll NEVER be able to hang them in the very same proportion to each other as they are in the real solar system."

David is able to read simple books on topics that interest him and lets you know that he reads parts of the daily newspaper at home. Board games are popular in your classroom, and David's specialty is chess. He not only shows a genuine feel for the spatial nature of the game but is also quite conscious that his playing skills are far above those of his classmates. Respectful of others, he doesn't seem especially pleased to win all the time, so you've suggested to his parents that he might join the after-school chess club. Recently he has started to be greeted cheerfully by much older children in the hall as your class heads to the library: "Hey David! You going to win again today?" Your sense is that his ability to "read" those he is playing against, no matter what their age, is an added advantage and an indication of his intrapersonal intelligence.

David may never have beautiful handwriting, but you are confident that, by nurturing his understanding of others and how the world works, he will continue to have positive experiences in his life—in school and beyond.

Naturalist Intelligence

Naturalist intelligence implies "expertise in the recognition and classification of the numerous species—the flora and fauna—of his or her environment" (Gardner 1999, 48).

Friedrich Froebel, the nineteenth-century "father of the kindergarten," possessed a naturalist intelligence, as his fascinating autobiography tells us. "My life was early brought under the influence of nature," he wrote, and indeed nature was the perspective that enabled him to face many life problems and challenges (Froebel 1982, 524). From his earliest years, playing in his father's garden, he felt a unity with nature that stayed with him always. It was strengthened when, in 1792 at age ten, he was sent to live with his uncle, in whose home free movement and liberty were allowed. Experiences as an apprentice woodsman at age fifteen reinforced his view of plants and trees as symbols of human life. When he finally realized that teaching was his calling, Froebel's concept of the unity of nature intimately connected with the way he viewed children—their physical and mental development and, above all, their need for spontaneous play.

Nearly two centuries later, the environmentalist and writer Rachel Carson made a tremendous impact on the world through her love of nature and through her efforts to help others see its glories and the dangers that threaten it. Her passion originated in childhood, as she explored the caves and tide pools of her beloved Maine coast, and she made every effort to bring to others the wonders and responsibilities that nature holds. In *The Sense of Wonder* she wrote:

> Down on the shore we have savored the smell of low tide—that marvelous evocation combined of many separate odors . . . of exposed mud flats and salt rime drying on the rocks. I hope [my nephew] Roger will later experience, as I do, the rush of remembered delight that comes with the first breath of that scent, drawn into one's nostrils as one returns to the sea after a long absence. (Carson 1965, 66)

Passing on her love for the wonders of nature, she also sought to alert us all to the dangers facing her beloved environment in her great cautionary book *Silent Spring* (Carson 1962).

In the Classroom

This year your class of fours and fives is an especially active group, so you've spent more time than usual thinking about outdoor activities that will stimulate and interest them. Your school's emphasis on recycling has inspired you to make a class trip to a local recycling plant, and the children's interests have been stimulated. They are beginning to understand that recycling is much more than sorting out paper and metal from other disposables, and there are processes involved.

Your snack program emphasizes healthy foods, particularly fruits and vegetables, so it's logical to begin thinking about starting a compost heap—or better yet, a worm compost bin! This will allow the children to put their leftover cores and peelings into the bin with some soil, and then to watch as the worms ingest, digest, and excrete the food to create new matter. The bin arrives, and you brainstorm the food recycling process with the children. There are "oohs" and "ughs" as the worms wriggle when the children add leavings from a juicy fruit salad snack. Fast forward six weeks, and the "oohs" and "ughs" have changed to complete silence, or "That's just disgusting!"

One afternoon you observe a small group of children, three boys and two girls, who belong to the "silent" group. They may be quiet, but they are riveted on the now fat and active worms. Day after day during outdoor time, they rush first to the worm compost bin and open the lid. If there's food to add, so much the better, but just watching appears to be equally fascinating. Two children in particular seem deeply engrossed, so before returning to the classroom you ask if they'd like to bring a few of the worms inside in a dish to inspect more closely. Minutes later, Jenna and Winton are sitting in rapt silence at a table inspecting the worms with magnifying glasses. You, aware that naturalist intelligence appears to be at work, quietly provide paper, thick lead pencils, and some markers, "in case you'd like to draw what you see." The results, quite delicate and detailed, surprise you and catch the attention of other children. Two budding naturalists have taken this recycling project from the observation of an interesting process through the initial stages of documentation.

The Intelligence of Big Questions

In his latest "candidate" intelligence, Gardner looks at what he calls "existential intelligence," "a facet of spirituality," or the "intelligence of big questions." This candidate intelligence is based on "the human proclivity to ponder the most fundamental questions of existence" (Gardner 2006, 20). I prefer to think of this kind of intelligence in light of the latter definition because I am so often amazed at the "big questions" small children ask. Rather than choose an example from the many famous spiritual leaders, writers, and activists such as Mahatma Gandhi or the Dalai Lama, I end this section with the kinds of big questions all of us as early childhood professionals hear from time to time. The first example is from a delightful little book by the Danish author and naturalist Carl Ewald, written about his three-year-old son.

> [My little boy] has an odd trick of seizing big words in a grown-up conversation, storing them up for awhile and then asking me for an explanation:
> "Father," he says, "What is life?"
> I give him a tap on his little stomach, roll him over on the carpet and conceal my emotion under a mighty romp. (Ewald 1924, 3)

The second example is one that was shared with me by Barbara, a graduate student and also the mother of seven-year-old Noah. Noah had many, many questions, so one day Barbara asked if she might interview him concerning the very big questions that were on his mind. Here is a partial list of Noah's big questions:

Why does life exist?

Why did God make us?

Whoever made God? Why did they make him?

If God had to be somebody, then how was that somebody made?

The sky has to stop somewhere, so what's the something behind it?

What is that thing behind it? Where does it stop?

How did everything exist? The sky . . . earth . . . how did babies come?

Did God make the solar system, or did he just make Earth?

Nobody could see gravity. If God didn't think of that, how was it made?

(I'm done, Mom!)

In the Classroom

Today is the day Grandma Rosa is coming to visit your classroom as part of a volunteer visiting grandparents program. Amy, a three-year-old of Chinese descent, sits quietly at a table by herself, intent on completing a fairly complex jigsaw puzzle. You watch as Grandma Rosa sits down on a low chair to observe Amy at work. A skilled preschool teacher in her time, Rosa does not comment on Amy's dexterity but carefully moves a puzzle piece that is about to fall off the table away from the edge.

"You have old hands," says Amy in a factual tone.

"Yes, I do," answers Rosa, "and I'm a grandma too."

"My grandma doesn't have white hair like you," comments Amy.

"Well, I kind of like my white hair," says Rosa.

To which Amy replies, "Yes, you're old. And then you'll be done."

Catching the last line of this dialogue, you head over toward Grandma Rosa and whisper, "I'm so sorry." But Rosa is doing all she can to contain her laughter. Later she tells you, "Can you believe a child of three can have opinions about such abstract thoughts as life and death, place them in a pragmatic context, and converse with you about them in a meaningful way? Now there's a child with big questions. Keep them coming!"

Using the Lens of Multiple Intelligences Theory in Our Work with Children

The lens of multiple intelligences theory allows us to expand our thinking and make it more concrete as we seek to understand children's differences in approach, their special interests, and their unique possibilities.

Multiple intelligences theory encourages us to be flexible in looking at the strengths of a specific child and the effect of children's specific strengths on each other as they function in a group. Take the example of a child who would much rather read or look at books all day than engage in an art activity or playground game with a classmate. If her classroom community allows for choice and promotes interaction, this proverbial bookworm may be drawn to the infectious enthusiasm of a boy who is illustrating his story or a girl who is industriously working on her kickball skills. Through exposure to the passions of others, our dedicated reader may begin to engage in other activities, discovering new personal strengths along the way.

Through this widened lens, teacher-caregivers, directors, and all of us who work with young children can become more aware of and attuned to each child's individual strengths. By expanding our skills in noticing children's ability to be stimulated by each other's demonstrations of intelligence, we will then find ourselves increasingly capable of nurturing every child's disposition to learn.

PROFESSIONAL DEVELOPMENT SUGGESTIONS

Assume that all the people described in the section on multiple intelligences theory are young children in your classroom. Create a list and schedule that show how you would provision your room and structure your day to accommodate these children's special dispositions. Discuss with a fellow teacher ways in which you could provide opportunities for them to share their interests and interact with each other.

Think about the children in your own classroom, and reflect on the interests they demonstrate and the possible intelligences each child possesses. If you're not sure, then take special time to observe those who don't stand out. Brainstorm with your director or a colleague about ways to encourage the children to interact and share their possible talents—without embarrassing them through excessive praise or inappropriate expectations.

Thinking About Part 1

Q What lessons can we take from an understanding of the young child's needs drawn from research of the developing brain and a developmental approach to early childhood education? How do these understandings mesh with consideration of family culture and societal challenges, and a theory of multiple intelligences?

A Perhaps the best answers can come from asking ourselves questions and using insights drawn from brain research to answer them.

Q Is it important for teacher-caregivers to have an understanding of how the young brain develops?

A Yes. We know how immensely active a child is from birth. Even though his brain is not visible and skills are gradually emerging, the drive to make sense of the world around him is nonstop. What's more, messages of all kinds—emotional, social, cultural, and physical—are having an impact as they are received by the young child from the surrounding environment with which he interacts— even though development may be progressing silently.

Q Does the fact that young children's heads are so loaded with brain cells mean that we'd better teach them as much as we can before they are three?

A No. An overload of facts and ideas does not imply that this input will have staying power. Children are learning constantly from their surroundings. It is important for them to use their own selective understandings, their own ability to put things together that make sense, in order to "prune away" extraneous information.

Q Is it important for us to be sensitive to children's cultural differences and the challenges they may face in their home environments as we observe and nurture the individual dispositions of each child?

A Yes. Consider the endless opportunities that lie in our increased understandings of family dynamics and culture for restructuring curriculum and encouraging children to share their interests with each other.

Q Is our recognition of each child's unique personality, social-emotional development, and demonstrated intelligence important for young children's growth and intellectual robustness?

A Yes. Nurturing young children's individual dispositions is centrally important to cultivating their disposition to learn.

Q Is a child's intelligence evident in only one way, such as a strong interest in music coupled with the desire to play an instrument or take singing lessons?

A No. A child may show her intelligence in several ways, such as a strong logical-mathematical talent combined with an ear for music and an interest in special games such as chess and checkers.

Q Should children who demonstrate the same particular intelligence always be grouped together?

A No. Exposure to other children and the variety of intelligences they demonstrate can only broaden interests and increase the capacities of each child.

Part 2

Perspectives on Practice

Inside Classrooms and Schools

Chapter 4

Environments That Invite Learning

Change and growth are goals not only for children, but for entire early childhood programs as well. As director of a college laboratory school for more than twenty years, I have been privileged to participate in change that was gradual and embracing—and now to watch my successor and her teachers bring the environmental aspects of the school to a new level. Change doesn't happen overnight. Change should not mean eliminating past concepts and practices that have served us well. Nevertheless, being open to change allows early childhood professionals to think dynamically about classroom environments that will tap children's possibilities and honor their dreams.

Learning from the Early Childhood Municipal Schools of Reggio Emilia

It was May 29, 1993, when I arrived as one of an excited group of early childhood educators in the small Italian city of Reggio Emilia. Presented with our schedule for the upcoming week, my roommate and I were both overawed and anxious about our stamina. Days began at 8:30 AM and ended in the early evening, combining three-hour lectures and visits to a wide variety of infant-toddler centers and preschools. Would we be able to make it, to give our visit the attention and concentration we knew it deserved from our discussions with colleagues who claimed they had been changed by the experience?

I had heard much talk among colleagues about the extraordinary capabilities of children in Reggio Emilia's early childhood municipal schools. Some of the comments were laudatory, while others were tinged with suspicion that the children were being explicitly taught adult techniques more appropriate for professional artists. There also seemed to be concern that art was an overarching focus that might slight other activities and materials important for children's development and learning. Instead, our group found an approach to early childhood education that complemented accepted practice in the United States and Canada. We also discovered a philosophic and pragmatic way of thinking about all aspects of early childhood education that stretched and enriched us as professional educators. Certainly some cultural differences existed and continue to exist today. The Reggio Emilia population is largely homogenous. Families pay minimum tuitions by our standards, and those in need are given special consideration. The concept of community, deeply ingrained in the culture of northern Italy, is played out in interaction between families, children, school personnel, citizens of the city, and members of the municipal government.

Now, looking back at my journal entries after more than a decade, I read the following:

> Sitting in this tiny restaurant, alone on the final free afternoon, I think about what I've learned. Personally I have been inspired to write a children's story based on a moving interaction between an Italian child and an American visiting teacher; to draw from life when I ran out of film; to speak some Italian when I thought I had no ear for language; it's clear that the poem "The Hundred Languages of Children" is relevant to the hundred languages of adults as well! Professionally I have learned to appreciate an eclectic, progressive, ever-changing approach to early childhood education that focuses on the essence of childhood, an image of the child rich in possibility, and the authentic meaning of "nurture" as it relates to teachers encouraging every young child's desire to learn.—June 4, 1993

Insights previously unexamined regarding my practice as an early childhood educator and specific aspects of Reggio preschool environments set new standards for me. Integrating these insights with the already-rich learning environments in my own school loomed as a challenge I would need to face.

A Reggio Perspective of Nurture and a Child's Disposition to Learn

The spirit of Reggio educators is one of openness to new ideas and interest in varying points of view. At the same time, classroom teachers, curriculum developers (*pedagogisti*), and resident artists (*atelieristi*) are passionate about their work and the principles that have developed from their years of refining the Reggio approach to early childhood education. Loris Malaguzzi, founding director of the more than thirty city schools, was a philosopher and educator who sought out the thinking of other early childhood educators, theorists, and psychologists from around the world. Basic principles as expressed by Malaguzzi and his dedicated colleagues relate directly to a specific concept of nurture—the belief that each child is born with the disposition to learn—and the need for environments that offer a wide range of opportunities to accommodate individual modes of learning.

The Image of the Child

Reggio educators see every child as full of unique possibilities from the moment of birth. A favorite metaphor is a series of photographs of an infant, Laura, in a high chair, examining her teacher's watch. As she shows Laura pictures of watches in a catalog, the teacher puts her watch next to Laura's ear to hear it tick. Baby Laura then suddenly plops her head sideways onto the catalog in order to hear the catalog watches ticking as well. The baby is making a hypothesis (something that looks the same must also sound the same). The implication is clear—young children must be nurtured through honoring their natural problem-solving capabilities and their desires to explore and discover. Thus, nurture does not imply coddling or overprotection, and it places the teacher in the role of facilitator.

The Rights of Children

Reggio educators understand that children have rights. First, they have the right to be children, to move about freely, to make their own choices from a wide variety of activities, and to pursue these activities in a time frame that is not, as Malaguzzi would say, "set by the clock." Among many other rights, children have the right to see their teachers as partners in the process of learning while still counting on them as reliable adults. They have the right to use all their senses as they explore and to enjoy the delicious smells of food cooking in the school kitchen. Every child also has the right to beautiful, inviting, and stimulating learning environments, evident in the design and provisioning of physical spaces. In these provocative environments, children can choose to work with a large variety of materials and, with the aid of teacher facilitators, to investigate questions that turn into ongoing cooperative projects.

Reggio Emilia Learning Environments

Entering a Reggio school is to be invited into a welcoming entryway leading to a central *piazza*. Based on the concept of a communal city square, the *piazza* holds many areas for children's play and exploration. The sound of enthusiastic voices fills the air, neither subdued nor out of control. Plants provide vibrancy and warmth. Large windows, mirror-lined triangles where two children may sit together, and light tables enhance the feeling of light and transparency. There are dress-up areas framed with wooden latticework where children freely enter and exit as they engage in choosing apparel and delight in the ensuing dramatic play their costumes inspire. There are "shopping" areas equipped with real food, a scale for weighing, a cash register, and a mini shopping cart. A comfy book area for small groups of children is found next to a basket of puppets and a puppet theater. Nearby stands a parent-built platform "dinosaur land," where a group of children engage in miniature world play. There are math games and puzzles and a large weaving frame with different colored strips of cloth with plenty of space for two to work side by side. Blocks of various sizes, including large hollow blocks, are neatly stored on shelves or platforms, drawing children of different ages to intermingle. A four-year-old girl works with intense concentration as she continues to build on a partially completed replica of New York City constructed from small colored cubes. She carefully assesses the placement of a block by checking the large photograph of the city mounted behind the emerging structures. In yet another area of the *piazza*, two five-year-old children work on a scale model of their school using pieces of wood and cardboard.

Encircling the *piazza* are

- classrooms for three-, four-, and five-year-olds

- smaller rooms for project work with clay, clay tools, and other art supplies ready for use

- a quiet room with musical instruments and a small table set up for two with watercolors and a vase of flowers

- an art room or *atelier* richly provisioned with art materials

- a well-equipped kitchen

Children move freely between indoors and outside, so some children are painting at an outdoor easel while others play on organic equipment such as a rowboat or a climber made of tires. At lunchtime, tables are drawn together in the *piazza*, and children help to set the tables with linens, china plates, glasses and tableware.

The Reggio Emilia *nido* or infant-toddler center that I visit is separate from the early childhood schools. One is welcomed by plants and light, but colors are gentle to the eye. There are carpeted spaces for beginning crawlers and walkers, and low climbing equipment. Cots and cribs are made up in soft colors, with swaths of draped material softening the ceiling. Each child has a notebook with notes and photos that travels between home and school, allowing parents to have a clear idea of what happens each day and the opportunity to respond. On the day I visit, a young teacher sits with a group of five infants and toddlers on a large sheet of paper where the children are experimenting by making marks with small pieces of pastel chalk. Occasionally the teacher will rub the mark (a pastel technique) to allow the color to spread on the paper. Nearby some toddlers have built a low structure atop a small platform with a reflecting surface—"provoking" one to wonder just where the blocks begin.

There is a joyous sound in these early childhood schools, where children and teachers engage exuberantly with each other and with their surroundings. The visitor is moved by the intensely human and respectful interchange between people of different ages and by the beauty of the environments.

Bringing the Reggio Experience Home

Arriving home to my own early childhood center, one with a long history as a college laboratory school for children ages two to six years, I was faced with a dilemma. How could I share some of the insights experienced in Reggio Emilia without undermining my teachers' confidence? As master teachers, their practice was seen as exemplary by parents, college faculty, and the National Association for the Education of Young Children (NAEYC) Academy for Early Childhood Program Accreditation teams who had visited us. We had a history rooted in developmental-interaction theory developed at Bank Street College of Education and a strong connection to our college's psychology department. Our Art of Teaching graduate program emphasized the concept of emergent curriculum. I wanted to think about change by examining the environments of our classrooms, but I realized that the first environmental change was my call. Our spacious front hall suddenly seemed terribly uninviting. Cubbies were old and shabby, the bulletin board was uninspired, and worst of all, there were no places for parents to sit! So I began by investing in some inexpensive but comfortable wicker furniture and a small rug. Then with the addition of some potted plants, the space quickly seemed more attractive. New cubbies would have to come under next year's budget. The bulletin board would be an ongoing project and might become a perfect place to begin displaying documentation of children's work—another key aspect of the Reggio schools.

The first staff meeting with my teachers focused on two ideas implicit in the Reggio approach that connected nurturance and learning—transparency and provocation.

Transparency

Many aspects of Reggio school environments evoke a feeling of transparency: large windows with a view to the outside and windows into classrooms; latticework frames that separate one area from another but allow visibility; mirrors and light tables. The Reggio concept of transparency relates to the idea that human beings of any age, gender, or ethnicity should be able to truly see through to and communicate with each other. If this is the goal, then there will be implicit respect on the teachers' part for the ideas and modes of children's learning. Children, in turn, will reciprocally respect and trust their teachers' understanding of them. A relationship based on the concept of transparency is key to nurturing individual children's disposition to learn.

Provocation

To provoke in the Reggio sense is to allow children access to materials and experiences that will stimulate their desire to learn. If provocation is taken into account in setting up learning environments, then there will be a variety of stimulating possibilities to accommodate each child's individual interests and dispositions. Provocation is also reflected in teachers' willingness to engage strongly with each other and their willingness to let children do the same.

   For our next staff meeting, the teachers asked to see slides of the Reggio schools I had visited, and then suggested we visit all of each other's classrooms. This experience was eye opening. It allowed the teachers to visit each other's classrooms and to receive input from their colleagues. As they began to critique and discuss the aesthetics and room arrangement of the different spaces, issues and questions quickly emerged:

- If, as Reggio teachers claimed, the environment itself should be seen as an additional "teacher" in every classroom, what changes would be necessary?

- Were there ways to introduce the ideas of transparency and provocation into the environment?

- Could we buy or build more bulletin boards to mount children's work in a way that would honor it?

- Where could we display documentation of projects so that parents as well as children would be able to examine and reexamine the thinking that went into the children's work?

As these thoughts and questions swirled around in our heads and in our conversations, it became important to first appreciate what we had and what we were already doing. Subsequent staff meetings gave us a chance to acknowledge our school's strengths.

Space

Our light-filled classrooms were thoughtfully arranged to allow for teacher supervision of children and easy movement from one area to the next. Some teachers were used to seeing furniture in a specific configuration or location but knew they had the autonomy to move things about depending on the needs of a particular group of children. For instance, if dramatic play with the wooden train set was a persistent favorite and spread out from the block area (where the trains were housed) into the dress-up corner, the teacher might reconfigure an intervening shelf to provide additional space for this daily activity. Or if playing "restaurant" developed into an ongoing interest, large hollow blocks to create tables and seating areas might be moved to a space adjacent to kitchen furniture, temporarily shrinking the size of the unit-block space and dress-up area but meeting the children's immediate needs.

We were fortunate in terms of outdoor play space. Our yards had climbing equipment and sandboxes, but also boulders, trees, and shrubs around which the children could dig in the earth and examine natural phenomena.

Materials

Our school was amply equipped with all of the basic materials essential for fostering young children's development. In every classroom one could see

- unit blocks carefully organized by shape on low shelves

- sand and water tables

- bookshelves or bookracks adjacent to a rug and soft pillows

- puzzles, math manipulatives, and tabletop building materials

- dramatic-play furniture and dress-ups

- crayons, markers, poster paint, fingerpaint and watercolors, easels, stacks of paper, and collections of materials for collage

- a workbench with real tools (for use under supervision by the older children)

Curriculum Projects

We were aware of attending to children's interests and had briefly discussed how curriculum projects might develop and be fostered. Assistant teachers, drawn from the Art of Teaching student body, regularly shared their readings on emergent curriculum with their lead teachers. As a staff we had read excerpts from Lilian Katz's and Sylvia Chard's writings on the project approach and watched a video on the evolution of a project. Some teachers felt they were already doing project work with children—for instance, one teacher always hatched chicks or ducklings in the spring—but there was some confusion about what the balance was between a teacher-introduced experience and a project that emerged from children's interests. Perhaps introducing the chicks was a provocation in the Reggio sense, and the children's questions, fueled by their excitement, could lead the teacher to alter or extend the hatching experience in ways she hadn't anticipated—thus transforming it into an emerging project.

Documentation

Our school valued teacher observations and samples of children's work to demonstrate individual growth over time. Every teacher was conscious of the importance of displaying children's work, even though we had never had a staff meeting directly related to the aesthetics of how to mount different kinds of work such as paintings, collages, clay objects, and built structures. However, our budget could not support an additional staff member, such as the Italian *atelierista* or art teacher, who might facilitate and advise us with display and documentation on a larger scale.

Learning to Be Comfortable with New Ideas

Over the ensuing months, teachers gradually began to make some adjustments and additions to their classrooms. As a staff, we attended a nearby Reggio conference and were inspired to hear presentations by Reggio teachers, directors, and art and curriculum specialists. One workshop, beautifully documented by *atelierista* Vea Vecchi, clarified our understanding of the term "projects." In this slide presentation, we saw a young child, perhaps four years old, working with clay and intent on creating a horse that could stand on its own four legs. No matter what the child does, the horse will not stand. In this case, the teacher suggests looking at something else with four legs, such as a chair, and trying to make a chair that will stand, before tackling the horse. In the process, the teacher introduces a clay technique that will help the child attach the legs. Other children wish to join the investigation, and soon a whole class is seen designing different kinds of chairs. After numerous tries, chairs stand, and eventually, so does the desired horse, along with myriad other splendidly unique horses. In this instance, the desire of one child to create a horse that could stand not only involved the teacher as facilitator along with an entire class of children but became the core of a project extending over time. Descriptions of this process in the form of dictated and written comments by the children attested to their persistence and learning that included understandings of proportion and balance, aesthetics, knowledge of leg positions of standing and moving horses (gained through viewing video segments of horses on the move), as well as language and literacy connected to the documentation.

Looking back, this was a period of questioning our thinking as early childhood teachers, similar to Jean Piaget's description of the disequilibrium children feel as they struggle to incorporate new understandings. It allowed us to become unsettled with the status quo, leading to a spirit of evolutionary thinking that continues in the school today. In the process, we learned that our belief in the central importance of dramatic play for social, emotional, and intellectual growth was shared by an approach to early childhood education that came from a very different history and cultural environment from our own. We discovered that we didn't need to give up closely held ideas in order to examine and enrich our practices. As we entered the twenty-first century, our school reflected a strong philosophical tradition alongside an enriched environment and an invigorated commitment to thinking about nurture as supportive of young children's learning.

A Visit to My Early Childhood Center

To illustrate the concepts of change and continuity, let's make a brief visit to the early childhood center I directed at that time and peek in on some classrooms where children are involved individually with a range of materials and activities. Please note: teachers' names have been altered for confidentiality.

Entering the School

As before, the hallway houses cubbies for the four-year-olds against one wall. But now there is a grouping of wicker furniture—a sofa and chairs covered in a colorful, patterned fabric—and a coffee table in front of shelves that house books for parents to share with their children before classes begin. A large bulletin board holds a selection of current articles on early childhood development and education along with announcements of upcoming activities. There are also a few pieces of individual children's artwork. On top of the cubbies, documentary panels show the fours' experiences hatching chicks. It is clear from this display, enriched with written commentary, that the teacher has expanded the experience by gathering information from the children about "what we know about chicks," candling the eggs, counting the days until hatching, caring for the live chicks, and finally returning them to the farm on a class trip.

Visiting the Twos

Twos teacher Laurel's strong aesthetic sense enables her to make the most of her semicircular, sun-filled classroom. A strong interest in art leads her to introduce two-year-olds to watercolor painting and collage, for which she provides glue and sturdy materials such as cardboard cylinders and pieces of wood. Walls display carefully mounted paintings with children's names. The teacher talks about sculpture as she watches the children work, shows them photographs of different types and sizes of sculpture, displays their work with care, and takes them to see an outdoor sculpture garden. She believes in order and appropriate materials for twos. Block shelves are stocked with basic shapes, and accessories often come in pairs to allow for two-year-old difficulty in conceptualizing the meaning of the word "share." The room is carefully arranged with

- a pretend-play area with minimal furniture but adequate numbers of sturdy dishes, a few dress-ups, and a doll bed with several anatomically correct dolls of different ethnicities
- a meeting area with book rack and circular rug with pillows
- an easel with poster paint, one or two colors at a time
- tables for playdough, puzzles, and other manipulative toys
- a water table with accessories

In the Reggio spirit of provocation, Laurel recently put multicolored marbles in the water table, only to be reminded by an accreditation team that the twos may swallow them! So, one now finds large, smooth pieces of beach glass, shells, and intriguing containers for pouring.

Visiting the Threes

It's lunchtime in the threes class, a favorite time for this teacher. Although she believes strongly in encouraging children's autonomy and competence, she has maintained a protective style of nurturing during meals, hovering over the seated children with a pitcher of water or a second helping of pasta. Thinking about differences in the description of Reggio mealtimes has been a challenge for Jeanine, until the day she entered my office full of excitement. "I've found some dishes I'd like to use instead of those thin paper plates that soak up spaghetti sauce! They're not exactly china—they're unbreakable—but they're simple and sturdy. And I've found bowls and serving spoons that I think will allow the kids to serve themselves!" On this visit to her room we see children setting out the plates, forks, and napkins, carefully counting one for each child. A yummy aroma of tomato sauce wafts in from the adjacent kitchen where children have helped prepare fresh pasta under Jeanine's supervision. When the two serving bowls of pasta arrive, one is plain and the other sauce covered. The children take turns helping themselves to their favorite preparation. Jeanine watches attentively, but her smile reveals genuine pleasure in the children's unique abilities and preferences around their selection of a favorite dish, and their growing levels of competence as they serve themselves.

Later in the afternoon two children are "cooking" in the pretend-play area. Realistic-looking plastic play food has been replaced with materials that serve as symbolic substitutes: a bowl of plastic bead necklaces, colored inch cubes, and a container of uncolored playdough. There are two rolling pins, pots, and some light metal dishes and utensils. The following dialogue demonstrates how a group of young children were able to represent food symbolically as they prepared a pretend meal.

JAMAYA: C'mon over and help me roll out this dough! We're gonna make spaghetti!

(Octavius and Bree join Jamaya and begin enthusiastically rolling out the playdough and cutting it into ribbon-like pieces with a play knife.)

JAMAYA: Hey! Ramon and me were gonna do that! Oh well . . . Okay . . . Ramon, how about this spaghetti that's already made?

(Jamaya picks up the necklaces and puts them in a pot one by one. Ramon points to some cubes.)

RAMON: And look, we can use these for our meatballs!

RAMON: How many for dinner? Let's set the table for all four of us—and we'll have two kinds of pasta, like Jeanine calls it!

Visiting the Fours

Marisol is an experienced teacher, confident in all aspects of her classroom program. Exposure to Reggio ideas, especially the staff attendance at the Washington conference, has caused her to question some well-established routines and to examine her classroom environment with new eyes. A formerly cluttered shelf, built into the wall, has been transformed with a variety of clear containers holding all sorts of objects for examining, counting, and sorting. Collections of colored pebbles sit next to jars of miniature pinecones and acorns and one jar with buttons of varied shapes, colors, and sizes. The effect is one of beauty. Marisol has had trouble mounting children's artwork in the past and was the first to request sheets of blue-gray bulletin board on her classroom walls to facilitate display. She has worked with colleagues to position individual children's paintings and collages for maximum aesthetic impact.

The effect is both calming and a pleasure for the children and their parents to visit. Instead of manipulative materials piled unappealingly in plastic bins, we see children bringing wicker baskets of materials to the tables or rug area. On one side of the new carpet for meeting time, there is a low platform with a rag rug and pillows. Two children sit there browsing quietly through a book from the hanging bookrack. In the building area, unit blocks are organized by shape along with new accessories such as small sandpapered birch-log pieces of different sizes. Miniature animals, sea creatures, dinosaurs, and human figures are available for dramatic-play scenarios on a table or in the water or sand tables. Clay is a new medium for Marisol, and she has been inspired to cut slabs of malleable clay and place them onto sturdy boards for the children to work with using simple clay tools. Small bowls of water are available to make slip (soft clay that facilitates adherence of one clay piece to another).

Today at group time Marisol is introducing "people color" paints, mixing them to match skin colors of the children in her class. She identifies the commercial color names such as peach and mahogany, but invites children's own versions of the mixed colors such as "peachy-chocolate." Using a brush, she paints a stripe on a child's hand asking, "Does it match? Do you think we need to add a bit more chocolate?" Later she will allow plenty of time for children's experimentation in mixing their personal colors for individual self-portraits.

Visiting the Fives

Dorothy is the only teacher who traveled to Reggio Emilia with me. A former elementary school art teacher, she is very sensitive to room arrangements that allow plenty of opportunity for individual choice. Although her classroom is relatively small, the dramatic-play area is appealing. Blocks and accessories are clearly organized. A round table designated for drawing and beginning writing is placed next to a shelf with different sizes of paper, coloring implements including crayons and broad and thin markers, and big round pencils along with medium three-sided pencils to allow for a firmer grip. A separate table for large construction projects, a workbench, an easel, and a light table (directly inspired by the Reggio trip) are available for children's choice. Near the meeting area, the bookrack is frequently replenished with books that reflect children's interests. Group projects include cooking, and Dorothy's confidence in the kneading capacity of small hands means that there is a frequent smell of homemade bread coming from her kitchen area.

Another group project, derived from the possibilities she observed in Reggio Emilia, demonstrates Dorothy's widened awareness of children's capacities. She and her assistant teacher have decided to introduce a year-long project centered on observations of the large tree behind the school. Armed with white paper attached to small clipboards, pencils, and thin markers, the children take sketching excursions to the tree. The results—every sketch unique yet reflective of the tree's characteristics at differing times of the year—astound the adults. The children themselves are intrigued by variations in each other's sketches. Soon, bark rubbings become a way to experience textural aspects of the tree's trunk. The colors of fall, the snow-covered branches of winter, and the buds of spring lead to important conversations about the tree as a living thing, the cycle of seasons, and respect for the environment.

Visiting the Kindergarten/First Grade

Sasha's classroom environment for the oldest children is provisioned with all manner of found objects and art materials positioned on low shelves. She has amassed a large collection of trade and reference books for the children to use. A carpeted block area invites both miniature and child-size dramatic play. There is a take-apart workbench for discovering (and occasionally reassembling) the inside workings of old radios, clocks, and computers; an easel for painting; and tables for project work such as making a papier-mâché volcano (emerging from recent news coverage of a volcanic eruption) or as space to practice "beautiful writing." The meeting area holds Sasha's rocking chair and an easel with chart paper. Here job and attendance charts are mounted at children's eye level. There are also a variety of graphs, a chart to record the "first hundred days of school" in rows of ten, posters, and samples of children's art work. The mounted lower- and uppercase alphabet is child-made and illustrated.

In this busy classroom, children begin to read and write as Sasha reads aloud to them. She introduces skills on the chart paper, making sure to involve the class in meaningful discussions of new letter sounds and digraphs, or punctuation marks they need to use in their own writing. There is also substantial time for the children to make choices, explore books, and play games, such as checkers and chess. Dramatic play is honored for these age levels as much as it is for the younger children, and a marvelous loft—handcrafted by a mother and given to the classroom—provides both high and low quiet spaces for conversation, reading, and play scenarios. The loft is a kind of gift of love, inspired by a parent's appreciation for the ways in which her child has been inspired to learn in this classroom. It is reminiscent of the Reggio parents' gifts of a handmade house for Barbies and a miniature dinosaur land made in response to children's interests and desire to engage in imaginative play.

Learning Environments That Welcome All Young Children Today

In the beginning there was a deep understanding of children's development. Teachers on the staff were educated and dedicated. Our budget was small. The children were both fascinating and inspiring—as they always are. Over the years, teachers retired, new teachers came, and directors changed. Educational perspectives and practice that brought a new focus to the importance of the environment enriched child development theory.

The center I once directed is now a delight for me to visit. It has been cited in a national magazine as a "model preschool early childhood center" (Hilgers 2006) through a new director's ability to add to and build on the previous openness to change. I would be remiss if I concluded this chapter on early childhood environments with directives, because without change, environments will become stagnant and uninspiring to both teachers and children alike. Instead, let the previous descriptions, professional development suggestions, and the photographs that follow provoke discussion and inspire ideas as you think about stimulating individual children's disposition to learn.

PROFESSIONAL DEVELOPMENT SUGGESTIONS

Each area of your center or school says something about your educational philosophy. Nurturing young children's disposition to learn will begin with a welcoming tone that invites family involvement. It continues in thoughtfully arranged classrooms where each individual child can find an entry point into the early childhood curriculum. Ask yourself the following questions, and list areas in your school or center environment that may need additional provisioning.

Is there a comfortable and pleasing adult seating area where parents or caregivers are welcome to spend time before the school day begins or before pick-up time?

Are cubbies, materials, portfolios, and charts organized for child and adult accessibility?

Is children's artwork respectfully displayed?

Is each classroom provisioned age-appropriately for the following curricular opportunities?

- building with unit blocks, big blocks, a variety of small blocks

- working with art materials such as clay, paint, crayons, markers, and chalk

- engaging in dramatic play with realistic or symbolic props, in child size or in miniature, both inside and outside

- experimenting with drawing and writing, using a variety of papers and tools

- exploring sensory materials such as water, sand, smooth/cooked playdough

- investigating science through observing and caring for animals or following the butterfly cycle; caring for the environment (growing plants, creating a compost heap); cooking

- playing games; putting puzzles together; working with creative and mathematical manipulative materials

- choosing from a wide range of picture books on different themes and interests

- sitting alone or with a friend, or meeting as a group in comfortable and comforting spaces

Read *The Diary of Laura: Perspectives on a Reggio Emilia Diary* by Carolyn Edwards and Carlina Rinaldi (2008). Have each teacher write a brief reflection on Reggio philosophy and practice as illustrated in this book in preparation for describing the Reggio approach at a parents meeting.

Early Childhood Environments That Invite Young Children's Disposition to Learn

Photographs by Margery B. Franklin

The following photographs, taken at the nationally recognized Sarah Lawrence Early Childhood Center, show learning environments that are carefully prepared to invite children's participation, investigation, and growth. The first photos will give you a sense of the thought and aesthetic sense teachers at the center invest in setting up their classrooms before children arrive. The ensuing photos show children throughout the day, spontaneously involved with materials and each other, engaging in symbolic play, and supported by teachers who take active as well as supportive roles.

We have presented the photographs together for easy reference, and hope that they will provide you with some new ideas and possibilities. Because they have been reproduced in a generous size, details are readily observable. This will allow the photos to serve as a source of discussion for college students studying early childhood environments and for directors and teachers in early childhood centers and schools focusing on classroom environments for purposes of staff development.

Welcoming front hall

Meeting area with book displays and portfolios

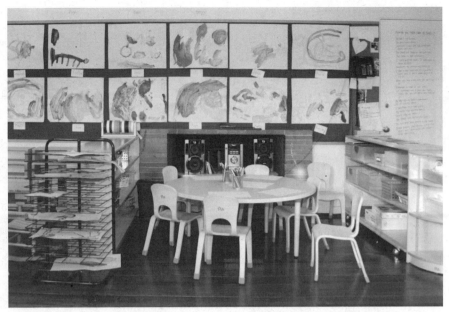

Center for drawing and writing

Children's cooking corner

Unit blocks and accessories

Dramatic-play props

Materials for "miniature world" play

Playdough setup with dough tools

Science discovery center

Invitation to explore music

Creating individual collages side by side

Concentrating on mixing paint colors

Investigating a new manipulative material

Exploring equivalency with large Cuisenaire rods

Combining large and miniature dramatic-play scenarios

Designing large play spaces with hollow blocks

"Cooking" on a hollow block "stove"

Working in miniature with playdough and animal figures

Supporting early writing

Engaged in independent drawing and writing

Using the senses in water-table discovery

Communicating ideas through water play

"How much sand will this bucket hold?"

"How many buckets did we fill altogether?"

Enjoying snack

Fostering beginning reading

Sharing a book with classmates at meeting time

Chapter 5

Observing and Describing

Observing and recording young children's behavior are a time-honored practice. Parents of today and yesterday (such as Nathaniel Hawthorne, author of *Twenty Days with Julian and Little Bunny by Papa,* and the nineteenth-century Danish writer Carl Ewald, author of *My Little Boy*) have kept diaries of their children's verbal interactions and activities as a way of remembering developmental milestones, individual differences and preferences, and those delicious, never-to-be-forgotten moments children inevitably give us. Teachers and teacher educators who understand the value of knowing each child advocate for written descriptions of children that are illuminating rather than judgmental. Not so long ago, narrative reports were a common mode of evaluation in schools, often more important than grades.

Beginning in the 1960s at the Prospect Center (1965–1991), a small school in Vermont, teachers and educational innovators looked for ways to make each child visible through observational inquiry. From their work, under the leadership of Patricia F. Carini, the Prospect Center's descriptive processes came into being. They provide frameworks for looking at children and their works, at teachers and teaching, and at classrooms and schools. The Descriptive Review of a Child was the first descriptive process to be refined and made available to a wider audience. Although it can be used throughout the grades, the focus here will be on its implications for early childhood teacher-caregivers and directors of early childhood programs.

It all begins with observation.

In "A Letter to Parents and Teachers on Some Ways of Looking at and Reflecting on Children," Patricia Carini writes:

> I have chosen a letter as the way to talk with you about looking at children and reflecting on what you have noticed for the reason that letters can be personal in tone and rather informal. And that fits with what I want to say about observing—an attitude or way of looking that I prefer to think of as "attending to children with care." . . . It is also important, though, to keep in mind that the purpose of attending isn't to scrutinize a child or even to "figure them out"—and certainly not to change them into someone else. The purpose is simpler and more ordinary: to be more sensitively attuned to who they are and are becoming, so that recognizing them as persons, we can better assist and support their learning. (Himley and Carini 2000, 56–57)

Observing and recording take practice, but they can soon become second nature. An exercise that Carini suggests is to regularly review one's impressions of a particular child to recognize more fully what you've already observed. Picture him in as many situations as you can. "Listen" to his voice in your mind. Keep a folder of notes and samples of the child's work. To capture observations on the go, it can be useful for teachers to think about some basic guidelines, from practical to the reflective.

1. Keep a small notebook or spiral notepad with you at all times. If it's small enough to fit into your slacks or apron pocket, all the better.

2. Practice writing while maintaining your attention on the child you are observing. Children are usually pleased rather than embarrassed about being noticed, and if asked what you are doing, it's fine to say something such as, "I'm really interested in what you're doing (or talking about)."

3. Insert a time notation at the beginning and end of your observation, and every five or ten minutes or so.

4. Note key words of a monologue or conversation so that later you will be able to reconstruct the words as accurately as possible. If a specific monologue or dialogue seems important, do your best to get as many of the actual words down as you can.

5. Be alert to the way children use their bodies as they engage in imaginary play and interact with materials.

6. Use language that is descriptive. Avoid assumptions (such as "She looked depressed") and labels (such as "He seems hyperactive").

7. Find a quiet time to complete your note and provide the classroom context as soon as possible after your observation.

The following description, based upon on-the-spot observations made by an assistant teacher named Devin, illustrates what can be learned from closely observing a child.

It is 9:15 and Carlo, age three, has just sat down at the playdough table. I watch as he surveys the materials at his disposal. The table has round mounds of playdough in front of each seat. Next to the playdough, in the center of the table, there is a container of brightly colored sticks, another container full of miniature plastic dinosaurs, and a third container that holds rolling pins and other kneading accessories. Carlo chooses one of the rolling pins and begins to press into his dough. He uses one hand at first, steadying the dough with his other hand. He manages to make the dough somewhat less thick; however it is by no means flat. Carlo appears not to be concerned with the flatness of the dough, and begins to work on the next part of his project.

Carlo's first task is to sort the dinosaurs out, and he chooses to group them by color. I notice that most of the colors he has selected contrast quite well with the bluish-green of the playdough. He picks up each dinosaur from his pile and places it within the dough, head up. I can now understand why the thickness of the dough may have been important—Carlo needed it to be thick enough in order to hold all the dinosaurs he selected within it. His main concern seems to be the placement of the dinosaurs, and the dough is simply a facilitator that allows him to accomplish this. Carlo sticks each dinosaur side by side into the playdough with the feet completely enveloped, and his pleased expression indicates that this is the effect he is trying to achieve. He then continues selecting dinosaurs and placing them until he has run out of space within the dough itself.

I wonder if Carlo is going to stop at this point, but to my surprise he continues working, building another layer of dinosaurs on top of the others in a seemingly random configuration. I no longer have a clear guess as to Carlo's desired result. Then I watch as he removes one dinosaur from those within the dough and places it next to the other "rejects" on the table. I ask him why he has removed that particular dinosaur and he pauses for a second, as if contemplating his answer. "That's a swimming dinosaur," he says, gesturing towards the creature's apparent fins. "He doesn't need to be on the dinosaur boat." All of a sudden it becomes very clear. The dull color of the playdough when seen next to the gleam of the table surface does indeed give the appearance of a "dinosaur boat." I then remember that Carlo brought a book to school this morning called *Dinosaur Train* and had been discussing it with the other children prior to his work on the "dinosaur boat." (D. Lipsitz, personal communication)

Devin's detailed narrative gives us a view of how three-year-old Carlo works with some malleable and specific materials and, with a few spoken words, provides insight into his learning process. It is clear that Carlo has well-developed hand-eye coordination for his age. He is able to plan carefully. He is able to sort in a logical manner, revealing a sense of color and an eye for detail, and he is able to represent the water (table surface) and the boat (playdough) necessary to provide needed elements in the creation of his "dinosaur boat."

The Descriptive Review of a Child

The format of the Descriptive Review of a Child is designed to enable teachers and parents to see—to understand—a child more deeply. It is not meant to highlight a perceived problem, but rather to reveal a child's strengths. In a child care center or elementary school where descriptive reviews are routinely used, the teacher will be just one part of the process. A colleague will chair the review, other teachers who know the child will attend (including a volunteer note taker), and the parents may be present. Samples of the child's artwork, projects, and writing add concrete elements to the review. In a formal review of this kind, the chair and the teacher will get together beforehand to frame the focusing question. This question is most often based on a teacher's desire to know more about individual children so that he or she can meet their needs. For instance, "I find too often that I'm not noticing Jasmine because she's so undemanding. How can I go about meeting her needs and seeing her in a more rounded way?"

To begin the review, the chairperson introduces the question and some basic facts concerning the child and the need for confidentiality. The teacher then presents her or his portrayal of the child under the following headings:

- Physical Presence and Gesture

- Disposition and Temperament

- Connections with Other People (Children and Adults)

- Strong Interests and Preferences

- Modes of Thinking and Learning

Following the presentation, others in attendance are invited to contribute. Everyone speaks descriptively and respectfully, and no one is interrupted. Finally, the chairperson pulls together insights and deeper understandings reached through this process of immersing the group in detailed, reflective language and description about the child. One of the extraordinary aspects of the process is the way a single descriptive review can illuminate a teacher's ability to observe all the other children in his or her class more clearly.

Observation that is descriptive and objective can only enhance the work of early childhood teacher-caregivers and program directors. Nevertheless, committing a center or school to participate in descriptive processes is a major undertaking and will include some personal choice.

Patricia Carini herself writes the following at the end of her "Letter to Parents and Teachers":

> What I have outlined above (detailed suggestions for observation and recollection under each descriptive heading) asks for a lot of thinking and reflecting. It isn't necessary to do this all at once, nor is it important if there are sections under each heading that don't ring any bells. Ignore them. Equally, this is an outline and there is a lot that isn't touched on. Add in anything that comes to mind—including other headings if that seems useful. Remember, this is an exercise and an organizing device. Use

it only in the degree that it is helpful to you in picturing the child and expanding your understanding of him or her as a person. (Himley and Carini 2000, 64)

One Early Childhood School's Use of Descriptive Review Processes

In a major metropolitan area, Children's Circle Early Childhood School for two- to five-year-old children uses descriptive processes as a way of sharing information with parents and also as a means of assessing its programs. Children's Circle describes itself in the following way: Parents are the child's first teachers and thus vital partners in early childhood education. Classrooms are rich in materials designed to encourage exploration and to support all types of learning. Interest areas exist in each classroom for block building, art, reading, water and sand, dramatic play, science, and math. The walls of the school are bright with children's artwork and personal stories. A large rooftop playground features safe climbing structures, a large covered sandbox, tricycles and other games, and a large wading pool in the summer.

The director of Children's Circle asks all teachers to write a descriptive review of each child in his or her classroom at the end of fall and spring semesters. Respect and attention to detail reveal meaningful portraits of the children that parents can appreciate, and also stand as documents of individual growth. The following descriptive reviews of children, one of a three-year-old boy and one of a four-year-old girl, vary in length and style; yet each gives us a vivid picture of the child presented.

Descriptive Review of Edward

PHYSICAL PRESENCE AND GESTURE
Edward is a 3.8-year-old boy of average height with a solid, slim physique. His thick, straight, dark brown hair frames his face, falling right down to his bushy eyebrows, and is a longer length in back down to his shoulders. He has wide, big brown eyes, strong facial features, and a charismatic smile. Edward wears bright-colored cotton clothing consisting of loose pants and T-shirts.

Edward enters the classroom at 2:00 PM with his mother. In his hand he carries a toy, usually a car brought from home. Edward easily settles into the rhythm of the classroom. His mother often stays as he wanders away to greet and socialize with his friends. Saying good-bye to his mother seems to be easier for Edward when she spends some time in the classroom.

Edward is a physical child who demonstrates physical control and agility when in motion. On the tricycle, his strong legs assist him in pedaling the bike around quickly, simulating a car or a moving train. He runs, climbs, and moves around the rooftop with ease.

DISPOSITION AND TEMPERAMENT

Edward is a social child who will, during the course of the day, play with all of his peers equally. He values his time with peers, and the children welcome his presence among them. Edward strongly cares about the other children's feelings and consistently shows empathy toward them. Whenever one of his friends is hurt or upset, he tries his best to comfort them.

Edward moves contentedly and confidently around the classroom with an almost constant smile and spontaneous bursts of heartfelt laughter. The following example illustrates Edward's humorous disposition. On this occasion, in response to Hank's riddle "Why did the chicken cross the road?" Edward responded, "Because there are no cars coming!"

Although he is an active child, running, climbing, and moving around the rooftop with ease, Edward seems to be equally content to sit quietly and contribute to a conversation.

CONNECTIONS WITH OTHER PEOPLE

Children and teachers gravitate to Edward's friendly and compassionate personality. During Late Day, Edward periodically approaches the teachers and inquires about snacktime, saying, "Not snacktime, right?" With consistent observations on the teacher's part, it has become clear that it is not the food Edward is interested in, but quite possibly what the food represents. That is, snacktime is a time when all the children congregate together and share a meal, similar to that of a family. Perhaps Edward's connection with his friends resonates with the warm interactions he experiences within his immediate family at home.

Edward is bilingual, and English is his second language. He has become quite fluent in English, honing his verbal skills by observing his peers as they engage with one another. It appears that the most important factor in his mastery of the English language is his need to provide verbal input in conversations and to communicate with his friends.

STRONG INTERESTS AND PREFERENCES

Edward's creative side is most visible at the art table. He tends to incorporate all of the tools available to him, and his illustrations are representational and detailed. For example, when he draws a truck he adds six wheels as opposed to the four wheels he will add when drawing a car. His depiction of a police car includes an antenna, a siren, and flashing lights. Edward's knowledge of motor vehicles is extensive, and this knowledge manifests itself in his drawings as he manipulates and utilizes the space of the paper by drawing distinct-sized cars and trucks at various angles.

Edward enjoys all the work areas of the classroom, but he tends to favor working with clay or playing at the dirt/sand and water tables. Edward will pound the clay, manipulating and shaping it to make miniature cars or large birthday cakes. At the water table, he is equally invested in washing baby dolls or pouring water through a funnel into bottles. At the dirt/sand table he tends to squeeze the dirt between his fingers and make balls or mountains with it. Edward will manipulate textured or pliable materials for long periods of time. When working with glue bottles in making a collage, he squeezes out all of the glue before adding accessories to the project. All of these activities strengthen his fine-motor skills as well as allow him to actively enjoy his friends.

Edward joins his friends as they build big vehicles with the hollow blocks. He also enjoys using accessories in the dramatic play that takes place in this area. For instance, he will put on a hat, grab a briefcase, and pretend to be going to work. He also likes to pretend-cook food such as pies, pasta, or cakes, which he then "serves" to the teachers and his friends—eagerly waiting for their reactions, probing a response by asking, "Did you like the food?"

MODES OF THINKING AND LEARNING

Edward shows a control of writing implements that indicates well-developed fine-motor skills. He holds his chosen writing implement in a loose pincer grip, in either his left or his right hand. He includes his wrist as he glides the writing tool effortlessly across the paper, never leaving the paper so that the entire drawing is made with continuous lines. At the easel, Edward will often paint over his work using many paint colors, and once finished he will say, "Oops! The car is crashed into the wall, and it is all broken now." Edward is able to transfer his mental vision onto paper, yet this does not dictate how he goes about exploring and quite possibly satisfying his hands-on experiences.

Two of Edward's friends have an interest in writing their names. Edward, who knows the alphabet, is able to recognize and phonetically sound out his friends' names and will assist the girls with their writing. One day, during Late Day, the trio spent a good portion of the time writing letters, with Edward leading the activity.

Edward is an active participant during circle time, whether the activity is reading stories, singing songs, or having a discussion. He tends to sit with his friends against the wall, cross-legged with folded arms. He is very attentive and asks meaningful questions that are relevant to the story or discussion.

Descriptive Review of Risa

PHYSICAL PRESENCE AND GESTURE
Risa is a solidly built four-year-old girl with brown eyes and short brown hair. She enters the room with confidence (this is her second year in the same classroom) and looks around to see what materials are set out and which other children have already arrived.

DISPOSITION AND TEMPERAMENT
Risa's social relationships are of utmost importance to her. With her friends she is playful and imaginative, even dramatic. Risa often serves as a catalyst, an inspiration, and a driving force for her friends as she engages in classroom activities, particularly in the dramatic-play area where you can often find her at the center of a maelstrom of activity, working collaboratively, elaborating ideas, and suggesting direction to play. When Risa shares an opinion or information about her own life, she does so with

a strong, confident voice. For instance, she has regaled us for some time now with detailed reports of her four-month-old brother.

Along with her social side, there is a part of Risa that values her privacy and time for introspection. This can be observed when she studies a book quietly, wants to play independently in private, or works intently on a piece of artwork.

CONNECTIONS WITH OTHER PEOPLE
Risa is good-naturedly receptive to her peers' ideas and automatically spreads and returns their enthusiasm. A best friend's idea for a sushi restaurant gets richly embellished and elaborated, inviting an increasing number of children into the orbit of the idea with Risa's infectious enthusiasm. Risa is an indispensable agent for sustaining interest in an activity and providing the necessary social lubrication for our classroom.

STRONG INTERESTS AND PREFERENCES
Risa's unique use of dramatic play reveals her way of making sense of the world, whether it is playing "family" or acting out a more complicated human interaction. Upon discovering a container of fabric, she excitedly explores its contents and almost immediately suggests a game of "clothing factory" with an available peer (with the afterthought, "for pirates"). With the help of her friend, she transfers the swatches of fabric over to the dramatic-play area along with some scissors and, conveying a mix of pretend and intent, starts clipping away. She first settles on the idea of making gloves and snipping holes for fingers in a square piece of cloth. Next she moves on to staple a "sweater" around her torso, eventually assembling the rest of her ensemble—including a scarf.

MODES OF THINKING AND LEARNING
Risa frequently prepares her workstation prior to beginning her work. She will stand in front of the art shelves looking for and collecting the desired materials, which she will relocate to her work place before sitting down. This allows her to put her attention and energy into the task at hand without having to make several trips to the material shelves.

Risa's artwork is often representational. She does not have limits on her artistic preferences and therefore will eagerly experiment with new materials. This can lead to her creating pieces of abstract art, such as three-dimensional sculptures and collages. At the end of the day, Risa carries an abundant amount of work home.

Children's Circle also uses descriptive observation to assess different aspects of the school's program. The following is a Late Day observation of children divided by age range into a little kids' room and a big kids' room. On this rainy day in November, a single longitudinal observation gives us a look at children enjoying dynamic Late Day curriculum in a relaxed setting that provides individual choice and group activity. The purpose of this review is to describe the classrooms in terms of activities, energy level, and general atmosphere.

Late Day Observation

Children came into Late Day at 4:00 PM, excited and energized to continue their morning work in the Little Kids room and eager to use crayons and paint also available for them to draw whatever they like. A group art project was also out for children to work on a canvas and add their input over a period of time, watching the project change. Children moved through the room and eyed an interesting mixture of color, paper, and tape with the freedom to add any combination of materials. The attraction to the art space was immediate, and so the class gathered around the art table and began adding handprints, brushstrokes, and layers of tape and paint. Pulling the tape and attempting to peel it off their fingers seemed fun and exciting. The challenge increased as the next attempt was to apply the tape to a surface wet with fresh color. Even so, the classroom environment was calm and relaxed. Girls and boys walked between the rooms in Little Kids, crossing in and out of art and dramatic play without feeling rushed or pressured.

The Big Kids room had a different level of energy. Volume was increased as many were shifting hollow blocks with whole bodies, using large movements to manipulate the shapes into a boat and a fire truck. Others were washing babies at the water table using sponges, cloths, and soap and water. Since rain was falling outside, there was extra time to work at the areas of choice. Instead of outdoor roof play, a parachute game was introduced. Classmates and teachers created waves with quick snaps of the fabric, providing wind sounds and simulating a boat ride in a wild, unsettled ocean.

After settling down for snack and free play, the big kids gathered together and, without being prompted, organized what seemed to be a big band complete with double bass, horn section, and lots of percussion. Some children thought their instruments were too loud, so teachers substituted pot drums with single xylophone blocks of a C scale. Some children noticed how the pitch increased as the xylophone pieces got smaller. Some would mimic the instrument tones with their mouths and would guess what the next piece would sound like.

In the Little Kids room there was music too. Their teacher brought out felt clothes and sang about "The Little Old Lady Who Wasn't Afraid of Anything." The class gathered together on the carpet, laughing and calling out as they tried to guess what article of clothing would be chasing the old woman next. Some children who already knew the song sat with friends nearby so that all could call out at the same time. (It was a moment where children were teaching each other as they participated together.)

As Late Day progressed, a relaxed atmosphere was palpable. The combination of age groups allowed for a rich atmosphere of sharing and helping one another. Both classes enjoyed the rainy day, the materials available to promote imagination, and also the company of teachers and peers. With all that was going on in both rooms, neither classroom felt cooped up. Children felt free to move, play, laugh, and learn.

Other Prospect processes include the Descriptive Review of Children's Works (often used in tandem with the Descriptive Review of the Child). These thoughtful observations of a child's work or collection of works such as drawings, paintings, sculpture, collage, or writing can bring tremendous insights to teachers regarding the individual child as thinker, maker, and learner.

Observation and description take time—personal and shared time benefiting individual children through the deepened understanding of adults who care for them. Teacher-caregivers and directors who carve time out of their demanding lives to do this work find that it allows for fresh and meaningful insights. To use Patricia Carini's words, it is the "art of seeing"—a clear, revealing, and enriching way of looking at children—that fosters the "visibility of the person" (Carini 1979).

PROFESSIONAL DEVELOPMENT SUGGESTIONS

Discuss the five areas covered in a Descriptive Review of a Child:

- Physical Presence and Gesture

- Disposition and Temperament

- Connections with Other People (Children and Adults)

- Strong Interests and Preferences

- Modes of Thinking and Learning

How does each of the categories help to focus the observations? What other categories might you suggest in addition to these five?

Have each teacher write a descriptive review of one child in her or his class, and present the reviews during a series of staff meetings. Discuss ways in which the reviews enable teachers to see all children in their classes more clearly.

As a staff, read a parent's observations and recollections of his or her child such as Hawthorne's *Twenty Days with Julian and Little Bunny by Papa* (2003). Discuss the reading as an inspiration to write personal reflections on your own child or a child in your personal life.

Read the poem "To Look at Any Thing" by John Moffitt from the collection *Teaching with Fire* (2003). Reflect and, as a group, discuss the poem's implications for looking deeply at individual children.

Chapter 6

Developing Positive Communication

Human communication, the understanding that occurs when people are making connections with one another, is a central element of our work with young children. Human communication is not only verbal but also conveyed through facial expression, gesture, and body language. For the hearing impaired, gesture and eventually sign language may take the place of spoken words. On an athletic court or field, communication takes place largely through whole-body language.

An easy way to put the importance of communication in perspective is to visualize the infant, unable to speak. What means are at the baby's disposal to alert the adults in her life to her needs? Hunger and discomfort manifest themselves through crying. Soothing voices, nursing, diaper changing, and holding communicate comfort in return. Soon our baby is responding with smiles and coos. The child's pointing directs our attention to her interests. Frowns and physical protests tell us what doesn't please her.

Jean Piaget's close observations of and interactions with his own children from infancy through their early childhood years advanced his understanding of the origins of knowledge and helped shape his theory of cognitive development. Incredibly detailed and objective on the one hand, his observations reveal a clear communication implicit in the infants' reactions to their own bodies, their environment, and their father's playful "tasks."

As infants become toddlers and talkers, language development plays an increasingly important role. Language and literacy researcher Catherine

Snow and colleagues describe the process in relation to children's eventual literacy learning.

> Adults try to understand babies' utterances as meaningful versions of their language, and babies appropriate what they notice in the adult language addressed to them and used around them. Soon, the structure of the child's sound system migrates toward the phonology of the language used in the community. The child begins to comprehend words and expressions from the language. . . . When a child has between fifty and two hundred words to use, morphological classes (such as nouns and verbs) and processes (for instance, suffix for plural) appear in their repertoire and syntactical structures (for example, subject-predicate sequences) organize words, phrases, and clauses for conventional semantic interpretation and pragmatic function.
>
> Early on, many toddlers love language events that highlight phonological patterns: songs, nursery rhymes, and games emphasize rhyming segments and alliterative patterns within and between words. As children participate in these language events, they start to exhibit phonological sensitivity, which can be a base for the phonemic awareness that is implicated in early alphabetic reading success. (Snow, Griffin, and Burns 2005, 17–20)

Communication, however, is not only verbal. By considering communication in the wider context of individual children's disposition to learn, we can see that responses differ and that emotions also play a significant role. Dr. Stanley I. Greenspan speaks and writes about positive communication between young children and the adults in their lives as the process of "opening and closing circles of communication." I was privileged to spend time watching and listening to Dr. Greenspan as he illustrated this concept during the making of a video project titled *Floor Time: Tuning in to Each Child* (1990). Sitting on the floor of the school I then directed, I saw Dr. Greenspan engage with a three-year-old boy, Adam, in one of our classrooms. As captured in the video, Adam looks silently at a selection of toy rubber animals. The circle of communication begins with observation, and Dr. Greenspan observes Adam for a few moments, then gets down on the floor next to him and begins to examine the animals. Talking quietly, he approaches by offering a toy lion to Adam and asking, "Would you like to shake his hand?" Adam shakes his head "no." Dr. Greenspan extends and expands the circle of communication by asking, "Could he shake your foot?" No. "Can he shake *my* hand?" Adam nods "yes." Dr. Greenspan then follows the child's lead, handing the lion to Adam and asking, "Does he want to stay with you or come back to me now? What do you think, Adam? Should he come back to me or stay with you?" Adam looks directly at Dr. Greenspan for the first time and hands the lion back to him. Dr. Greenspan thanks him warmly, and so this circle of communication comes to an end.

The more opportunities children have to interact with adults and with each other, the richer their communication skills will be across the domains of expression.

Communicating in Your Personal Voice

Temperaments may differ, but all of us who work with young children know that positive communication with the children, their families, and our colleagues is a necessary aspect of our chosen profession. The first step in thinking about positive communication is to realize that each of us has a unique voice. I remember my own student teaching placement with Erna Christensen, a master teacher of first and second grade. I adored this gentle woman who was so generous in her encouragement of me, and I marveled at her ability to maintain children's attention with her consistently modulated voice. No matter how hard I tried to emulate Erna's style of communication during my first year of teaching, I could never get the same controlled reaction from my class. One day I (metaphorically) threw up my hands and gave myself a talking to. "That's not YOU, Sara! Your voice isn't naturally that soft, and you like a louder classroom—not an out-of-control classroom, but one that has a good hum going. Try to be yourself!" This was a transforming moment for me, and from then on I began to feel comfortable in my work with children.

Communicating with Children

If you are a naturally quiet person or teacher, it doesn't mean you won't be able to reach all the children in your class. You'll do it in your own personal way, and they will respond to you as the gentle person you are. If you are a boisterous person, you may need to tone down your strident side, but your enthusiasm will communicate itself to your class and be appreciated.

Visiting other teachers' classrooms over the years, I have heard many different voices. Despite differences in style, the classrooms that stand out in my mind are those in which the teacher speaks to children as equal human beings. This does not mean that she relinquishes control of the classroom, nor that children believe their teacher is another child. In fact, children feel unsafe with adults who set no boundaries. Rather, there is a tone in the teacher's voice that is direct and respectful. In addition, there's a way of listening that imparts an unspoken message about the importance of people communicating with each other. The example below follows Sallie, a dynamic teacher with a direct (though not directive) style, from a classroom transition to group time.

(Sallie has had a busy morning with her four-year-olds, who seem to have caught "spring fever," and pulling them together for a group read-aloud is a challenge.)

SALLIE: Ali, could you please put those stray blocks back on the shelves? Bashia, I know you want to keep your building up, but let's clear space around it for tomorrow—and so no one will trip. Jen and Gus, there's an awful lot of scrap paper left on the collage table. Can you get it together in the basket?"

ALI: Sallie, I want you to read the book I brought from home—nobody else's!

MAGGIE: No! She promised me to read *Frederick!*

SALLIE: Whoops, people. There's so much noise I can't hear you clearly. Come on over, everybody, and let's decide on a story together.

(Jake and Kayla start setting out snack for the class as other children gather on the rug.)

SALLIE: Can everyone hear me, even the snack helpers?

(Sallie had already chosen *Abuela* to read this morning because Francisco's grandmother is visiting from Puerto Rico, but she now faces issues of the other book suggestions, adequate time, and four-year-old staying power.)

SALLIE: We've got so many books I could read, but I know you want to go outside after snack. How will we decide? I already picked *Abuela*, but Ali brought in *The Very Hungry Caterpillar,* and Maggie reminded me I promised *Frederick*. So, what shall we do?

(Loud chorus of voices promoting different books.)

SALLIE: Okay, hold it! You want them all, so here's what. I'll read *Frederick* because I promised, and maybe *The Very Hungry Caterpillar* if there's enough time. Then after outside time we'll read *Abuela*.

FRANCISCO: Yeah! Because my *abuela*'s here!

JEN: What does *abuela* mean?

SALLIE: Francisco, can you tell us?

FRANCISCO: It means grandma! Granny! In Spanish!

GUS: Last year sometime my mom made Spanish rice, and I hated it! And guess where I'm going after school today? To the zoo! With Mom!

SALLIE: You're going to the zoo after school, Gus . . . and you had Spanish rice and you didn't like it. But maybe one day we can make Spanish rice in school, and Francisco's *abuela* can help us. Right NOW we're going to hear *Frederick!* (Begins) "All along the meadow. . . ."

In this somewhat unpredictable interchange Sallie never loses her tone of respect. Her voice is warm, and by turns firm and humorous. The children trust her willingness to listen to them. She is involved in the conversation. She holds to her plan of reading *Abuela* but keeps her promise and values the home-school connection by agreeing to read a book brought from home. She wonders along with the children about the meaning of a Spanish word, while accepting off-the-cuff comments about Spanish rice and a trip to the zoo. Sallie is communicating with her class as an equal person, but also as a teacher who invites suggestion and helps make decisions.

Communicating with Colleagues

The communication skills we practice with children aren't always equaled by our communication with colleagues. Of course a collegial school atmosphere is in part the director's responsibility. The director serves as a role model for all the adults who work in a center or school, as well as for the adults who bring children to her program. Many of the qualities we seek in our work with children are equally meaningful in these adult relationships—respect, warmth, a serious approach to work, and appropriate humor head the list. Trust may take more time to achieve but remains a worthy goal. All these qualities, together with occasional firmness, are part of the director's range of authority and concern.

One way to think about the ingredients of getting along with colleagues is to examine what I like to call my "Five Cs of Communication."

Conversation: the act of people talking together; a way to connect

Collegiality: giving the other person a break; smiling, listening, providing constructive feedback

Cooperation: willingness to work with others; taking at times either a leading or a secondary role

Collaboration: taking the time to build communal knowledge through discussion

Confrontation: accepting that challenge and conflict can be positive rather than adversarial; finding non-aggressive ways of talking that lead to bigger ideas

With the Five Cs of Communication in place, the addition of a sixth C—Community—is possible. Time is always an issue, so brainstorming to find best times and places to communicate is key. Ask yourself the following questions:

- What times of day are most conducive to getting together?

- Under what circumstances and where should we meet?

- What are the most important things for us to talk about?

At a recent workshop, I was intrigued to hear a director say, "The best time for us to meet is first thing in the morning. Everyone arrives early, an hour and a half before the children are expected, and sets up their classrooms. I have breakfast waiting, and unless there's an urgent problem—a family issue or a child in distress to discuss—we talk about what's *working* in our classrooms. That day (every two weeks) is just the best day for all of us!" Other schools may feel more comfortable with an after-school staff meeting, and topics related to a specific curriculum area or a book the staff has read together. Arranging for teachers to visit each other's classrooms is another powerful way to enrich community through interest and empathy. Whatever the means, practices that increase positive adult communication should be decided on by staff and administrator together.

Communicating with Families

Family-teacher communication begins on day one of each new school year—and even earlier if the program endorses prior home or school visits. We have seen in chapter 1 that the basic role of nurture on the part of teacher-caregivers is central to the healthy development of young children. Nurture, however, must also extend to the families who are entrusting their children to us for a large portion of their waking hours. It's hard for parents to be separated from their children, no matter how this manifests itself on the surface—sometimes so hard that denial is necessary. The mother who dashes into school and leaves without a kiss the instant her child seems involved may be in as much distress as the one who lingers. Having a clear separation policy is therefore an essential element of every program. An attitude of "out of sight, out of mind" is not just a false concept, but actually harmful. Families need help in honoring the deep feelings both they and their children are coping with during the leave-taking process.

Over the years I have observed a wide range of coping behaviors around separation. Indeed there were parents, grandparents, and trusted family caregivers who quite quickly and easily left engaged children in classrooms at the start of the year. There were also occasions when family members left abruptly, and children languished, unable to become interested in classroom materials, activities, or peers. In such cases, I would ask the adult to return and, depending on the age of the child, to determine whether this seeming lethargy was an indication of separation anxiety or a thus-far unexplained phenomenon. Then, there were adults who found it nearly impossible to be clear about leave-taking, resulting in loud crying on the part of the child. In this latter situation, I learned to read those cries fairly accurately (though not infallibly).

If my gut told me, "I think this is more an adult issue than a child issue," the teacher, family member, and I would work out a plan together that went something like this: after a good-bye hug from the parent and assurance of return at an appointed time, the teacher holds and comforts the child as I guide and comfort the adult out of the classroom and building, assuring her that I will call if the crying does not abate. Most of the time this strategy worked. When it didn't, we would request that the adult remain with the child in school for a while longer.

In each family situation, the overriding goal is to provide support. This is true in supporting children and families as they make a comfortable transition to school, and becomes even more important as the ongoing work of staying in communication continues. Modes of communication will vary based on the school or center policies on parent-teacher conferences, informal contact, journals that travel to and from school, and structured or unstructured classroom visits by family members. As long as the teacher-caregiver is willing to communicate—her tone warm and welcoming, her attitude uncritical—most families will relax and be able to appreciate their individual child's school experience.

Children Communicating with Each Other

The structure and philosophy of an early childhood setting conditions ways that children communicate with each other. Single-age and multi-age grouping, classroom structure and setting, and the flow of communication throughout the day affect possibilities for communication among children.

Single-Age and Multi-Age Grouping

In the schools of Reggio Emilia, infants and toddlers usually occupy separate schools designed specifically for them. While respecting the potential of every child, these schools feel quieter because of the onset of developing language. Teachers warmly interact with these young children, carefully observing their gestures and expressions, encouraging their efforts. Threes, fours, and fives are grouped together in the same building, but have separate classrooms where they begin the day with their teachers and to which they return at different points in the day. However, the central piazza (around which the classrooms, *atelier,* and mini-*ateliers* are set) allows for free interchange among all the children for significant periods of time. These schools make a dynamic impression as children of varying ages interact in the *piazza* or out-of-doors in dramatic play and other open-ended activities.

In our country and other parts of the world, multi-age grouping can be seen in Montessori schools for three-, four-, and five-year-olds, programs based on the British Infant School model, and even in some private and public primary schools. One advantage of multi-age grouping as a facilitator of positive communication lies within the structure itself. Older children who move on to another class are replaced by a new and younger group, but there is always a middle core that remains. In the case of a kindergarten-first grade or first-second grade, a consistent core will exist if the teacher remains with the class. In these scenarios, children who stay in the same classroom for more than a year already know each other, communicate easily, and can welcome the newcomers to their community. An additional advantage exists if members of this core group have been empowered to speak out and challenge each other in a positive way—a guarantee of lively talk from the get-go.

Effects of the Classroom Setting on Ages and Stages of Communication

In chapter 4, we considered the importance of learning environments that meet the disposition of every child. Looking beyond the environment to the individual and to the group leads us to an important word: choice. A classroom structured to invite choice fosters individual interests while at the same time inviting group communication. Along with adequate time for children to delve deeply into their activities, choice will necessarily affect the amount of positive communication that results as others join in.

Twos and threes tend to do best if they enter the classroom without the formal expectation of a meeting or group time. Some will make a beeline for their favorite activity, often a way of becoming comfortable. Others will stand and watch for a while, thinking, "What's the same?" "What's different?" "Who's here?" Attention spans tend to be short and dramatic play fluid. Children come and go at their own pace, sometimes leaving the block area after a few minutes, at other times working next to other children with concentration. Communication is happening, but in a subtle manner (or not so subtle, as in grabbing or hitting). "Use your words!" the teacher says, and the more ways she finds to express this, the more impact it will have. Language is emerging and growing by leaps and bounds. Children are striving to connect. The communication process is evolving.

Fours and fives are eager to begin the day with a meeting time when they can take turns sharing their experiences outside of school. Teacher-led activities may include children recognizing and placing attendance cards on a chart, reviewing jobs, and discussing the calendar and the day's weather. But the most interesting focus will be on activities available in the classroom and the children's preferences regarding where to begin. Choice of activity may be restricted for a while because of excessive numbers in each area, but soon converging interests—working and playing side by side—will result in lively conversation. Outside play brings different children together around imaginative play or an active game. Later at a group meeting, these same children will be eager to listen and to share with each other if given enough time to delve deeply into their joint activities. At a point when elementary schools are concerned with prekindergarten and kindergarten children's perceived lack of listening "ability," it's good to remember that the kinds of practice provided by the above examples of positive communication will serve these youngsters well.

For teachers at every age and grade level, positive communication is a sign that children are learning from each other. Looking back at myself as a novice first-grade teacher, I remember the moment I decided to step back and trust my six-year-olds. As they made their own choices in the room I'd carefully prepared, interacting freely without the pressure of time, a productive hum of questions and conversation emerged. I circulated around the classroom. I listened, and I learned what good thinkers, speakers, and listeners these children were. This moment was a turning point in my own career, a more significant lesson in classroom management than any I'd learned in my teacher education program.

Communication throughout the Day

Children's voices change with the ebb and flow of indoor and outdoor activities. There is spontaneous talk, the involved sound of children working side by side in a productive way. There is quiet talk at snack, lunchtime, or before rest. There is loud talk that goes hand in hand with large-motor activity and the sheer pleasure of being outside or in an unrestricted space.

Following a teacher and children through a typical schedule of a full-day program can provide us with a sense of the embedded opportunities for communication inherent to each part of the day. At Children's Circle, it looks like this.

8:30–9:00	Children arrive during an unstructured time, as teachers greet each child and accompanying adult and facilitate separation issues. The tone is relaxed. A crying child may need to be comforted, but this is seen as an opportunity to connect.
9:00–9:30	The fours and fives have a class meeting. A welcoming song such as "Here We Are Together" acknowledges all the children who are present. Attendance, jobs, calendar, weather, and introduction to available materials and projects are discussed. Children share significant news from home that's on their minds.
9:30–10:45	This is a choice-work time with special projects and free access to all areas of the classroom. The teacher observes, facilitates, and encourages as needed.
10:45–11:00	Cleanup time. Children and teacher participate together.
11:00–11:20	Snacktime. This is a time for quiet conversation.
11:20–12:00	Outside play on the roof. Although it's wonderful to have a yard where children are able to investigate the natural environment, this is beyond the capacity of many programs. Trips to a park or playground may substitute. At Children's Circle, teachers observe their children's play on the roof. Loud voices are natural avenues for communication during this active time.
12:00–12:20	Story time. This is precious time for communication through listening and responding.
12:20–12:45	Lunchtime.
12:45–1:45	Rest time.
1:45–2:00	Wake-up time, followed by snack.
2:00–6:00	Afternoon and Late Day programs follow the morning schedule, with the exception of lunch. There is an extended story and music activity during this period. As the afternoon progresses, children can become a bit crankier, anticipating the end of the school day and reentry into the home. Activities are more fluid in terms of specific time periods, and teachers may become more playful in their interactions with the children, seeing this as a way to ease the transition to home.

In schools and centers where positive communication is a major goal, all members of the community will be conscious of its importance. Children and adults will be increasingly open to each other as they experience acceptance of their own personal ways of making connections. In the realm of human communication, it matters little whether you are quiet, boisterous, or thoughtfully conversational, or if you are a child or an adult. What does matter is this: in an atmosphere of respect and tolerance, human communication is bound to flourish.

Finally, remember to take care of yourself. Good communication skills are demanding, even when you've reached a point where you know your style and how best to use it to connect with others. When the day has been tough or you've had a frustrating parent-teacher conference or feel you've failed—forgive yourself! Being a teacher-caregiver or a center director is one of life's hardest jobs. If the class energy has worn you out, give yourself a little personal downtime or seek out a colleague for some TLC. While complaining can tire you out, reaching out to others for comfort will please them and bring you relief.

PROFESSIONAL DEVELOPMENT SUGGESTIONS

Think about a child in your classroom with whom you have difficulty communicating. Is she a child you think of as difficult or perhaps a child who seems to lack self-control? Do you hear yourself frequently calling out her name in an effort to stem acting-out behavior? Make a list of your responses, and evaluate those that seem focused on her negative behavior.

With the help of colleagues, develop a framework for thinking about approaches that seem to reach a child you find difficult to work with. Does he respond to humor? To touch? Ask yourself to reflect on his interests and which materials "turn him on" in a positive way. Are there things you like about him, and do you let him know you notice when things go well? Make a list of your strategies, and use them with this child.

If you are concerned that a child in your class is "too good," view the child's behavior through the same lens as you did with the child you found difficult. Just talking about a child from a different perspective can open up possibilities for connection. Write down your observations, and share them with your colleagues.

Chapter 7

Standards, Curriculum, and Young Learners

A parent told me recently that what she wanted from her child's school was evidence of progress from one day to the next. As she assured me that all the parents she knew felt the same way, I experienced a wave of sympathy for their dilemma. Young children do not demonstrate progress on a day-to-day basis. Yet in a climate of standardized assessment, adults feel pressured to be sure their children are receiving the necessary tools to achieve identical goals at identical times. The flaw in this reasoning lies in the denial of children's individual differences and the fact that learning is a process. If early childhood educators respond to parental anxiety, we run the risk that a continuous flow of photocopied activity sheets will be sent home as false "proof" of progress and a misinterpretation of meaningful learning.

Recognizing and Coping with the Risks of Standardization

Parents as well as teachers know instinctively that children express their intelligence through a variety of avenues. They also know that children develop varying capabilities at different times. Despite this, it's easy for parents to be unsettled by the notion that arbitrary standards will be applied to their unique children and that emerging skills will be evaluated on the basis of arbitrary benchmarks. The National Association for the Education of

Young Children (NAEYC) in a joint position statement with the National Association of Early Childhood Specialists in State Departments of Education (NAECS/SDE) endorses early learning standards while cautioning us about the risks:

> The major risk of any standards movement is that the responsibility for meeting the standards will be placed on children's shoulders rather than on the shoulders of those who should provide opportunities and supports for learning. This risk carries especially great weight in the early years of schooling, which can open or close the door to future opportunities. Negative consequences potentially face children who fail to meet standards, because data may be used to label children as educational failures, retain them in grade, or deny them educational services. Culturally and linguistically diverse children, and children with disabilities, may be at heightened risk. (NAEYC and NAECS/SDE 2002, 3)

When rigidly applied and assessed by standardized testing, early learning standards ignore the fact that young children already possess personal standards that they set for themselves, and personal progress, separate from the benchmarks set by exterior standards, is invisible.

Personal Standards

Recognizing a child's personal standard is not difficult if we are on the lookout for it. Drawing and beginning writing are obvious areas for observation. Jake, a four-year-old with a passionate interest in dinosaurs, wanted to draw a tyrannosaurus rex. After several attempts, followed by fierce crumpling of paper, his teacher took him to the center's library where they picked out several books on dinosaurs. Jake looked intently at the pictures, tears running down his face, and then said, "I just can't draw that well!" Later in the year, following a read-aloud from Ruth Stiles Gannett's *My Father's Dragon,* Jake was excited about attempting to draw a dragon picture using both lead and brightly colored pencils. He carefully outlined his dragon in lead pencil. Hesitating, Jake looked up at his teacher, and then began to work in color. The final result not only pleased him, but elicited enthusiastic praise from his classmates.

Personal Progress

More than twenty years ago, British educator and language researcher Gordon Wells warned his readers to beware of equating achievement with progress.

> Measurements of achievement are almost always made with respect to a group of children of approximately the same age. They are therefore biased against slow developers who, by definition, achieve low scores relative to their age peers. However, it does not follow at all that because a child remains at the bottom of the class throughout a year or even several years that he or she has made less progress than the child who was consistently at the top of the same class. . . . Always coming off worse in age-related comparisons of achievement, they may easily come to be seen and to see themselves as intrinsically less well able to learn and, as a result, cease to make the progress of which they are capable. (Wells 1986, 138)

If, however, children are given time to develop, the resulting success will be empowering. Chrissy, a five-year-old with a somber and methodical approach, loved to practice letter formation and was intrigued by letter-sound relationships. This focus on letters and sounds enabled her to write well-structured stories, using inventive spelling, on topics that were interesting not only for her but for other children. At the end of her kindergarten year, having just turned six, Chrissy was still a struggling reader. Her very strong phonics skills actually impeded her reading as she struggled painfully to sound out each separate word. In the summer between kindergarten and first grade, a relaxed time without tutoring, something began to "click" for Chrissy. She entered first grade tentatively, but before the first parent-teacher conference in November she announced to her mother, "Well, you *know* I'm good at math. And you *know* I like to write. But I bet you don't know I'm the best reader in the class!" And it was true. If Chrissy's reading comprehension had been assessed at the end of kindergarten, she might have been relegated to a "low" reading group in first grade, and the remarkable progress she made in just a few short months would not have been visible.

Creating the Conditions for Success

In their excellent document, "Early Learning Standards: Creating the Conditions for Success," NAEYC and NAECS/SDE (2002, 4–8) cite four important elements without which early learning standards will be meaningless. This document, which continues to be updated, consistently includes these elements and is endorsed and supported by the American Academy of Pediatrics, the Council of Chief State School Officers, and the National Association of Elementary School Principals.

These elements, or essential features, are the core of a developmentally effective system of early learning standards.

1. "Effective early learning standards emphasize significant, developmentally appropriate content and outcomes" (NAEYC and NAECS/SDE 2002, 4).

   This element translates into an acknowledgment of the whole child; meaningful learning activities and experiences; standards that are not watered-down versions of grade-school curriculum; recognition of developmental stages; and accommodations for differences in children's cultures, languages, communities, individual characteristics, abilities, and disabilities.

2. "Effective early learning standards are developed and reviewed through informed, inclusive processes" (NAEYC and NAECS/SDE 2002, 6).

   This element requires the development and review of early learning standards through relevant and accepted sources; the involvement of community, families, early childhood educators (including special educators), and other professionals; shared discussion among all stakeholders; and regular review and revision of the adopted standards.

3. "Early learning standards gain their effectiveness through implementation and assessment practices that support all children's development in ethical, appropriate ways" (NAEYC and NAECS/SDE 2002, 6).

This element stresses that young children's interests and abilities must considered in curriculum, classroom practices, and teaching strategies to promote positive development and learning. Assessments must clearly connect to the standards and provide useful information while remaining technically, developmentally, and culturally valid. Assessments should be used to improve practices and services, benefiting from rather than merely using information to rank, sort, or penalize young children.

4. "Effective early learning standards require a foundation of support for early childhood programs, professionals, and families" (NAEYC and NAECS/SDE 2002, 7).

This final element requires program standards to have an evidential base and enough resources so that high-quality programs can implement the standards effectively, significant professional development to help early childhood teachers and administrators with implementation, and respectful family communication and support to allow the program standards to achieve maximum positive effect.

Connecting Early Childhood Curriculum to Early Learning Standards

Each state is responsible for articulating early learning standards, but it is the responsibility of school districts to adapt and adopt them through a process that takes the NAEYC and NAECS/SDE elements into account. The next step is to develop and implement an early childhood curriculum that respects both the standards and meaningful learning for young children.

Because each state expresses early learning standards using different terminology, a book such as Gaye Gronlund's *Make Early Learning Standards Come Alive: Connecting Your Practice and Curriculum to State Guidelines* (2006) is an invaluable guide. Her identification of seven discrete early learning standards embraces the range of standards adopted by states throughout the United States—literacy, mathematics, science, social studies, social-emotional development, physical development and health, and the creative arts. By describing and illustrating each standard "in action," Gronlund demystifies the large subject matter areas, making them accessible and relevant for early childhood educators.

Literacy: Examining One Early Learning Standard from Top to Bottom

Literacy is perhaps the hottest topic in relation to standards and their implementation at all age and grade levels. Beginning at the top allows us to project how state standards for literacy (or English language arts) might be interpreted for purposes of curriculum development, instruction, and assessment in a prekindergarten program in a public school district or in a private early childhood center or school.

Overview of One State's Literacy Standards

Let's look at a hypothetical state that has four literacy strands we need to address.

Standard 1: Language for Information and Understanding

Standard 2: Literary Response and Expression

Standard 3: Critical Analysis and Evaluation

Standard 4: Social Interaction

In one of the state's public school districts, a committee comprising a diverse group of early childhood (K–2) teachers from the district, local early childhood program administrators, and college teacher educators gather to share their expertise in designing a new prekindergarten program that follows state standards. The committee members agree to tackle the literacy curriculum first. The process evolves as follows:

- The committee members keep in mind a time-honored definition of literacy as speaking, listening, reading, and writing. These classic elements of literacy curriculum connect and sometimes overlap within each of the state standards. (For example, Standard 1, Language for Information and Understanding, is addressed by classroom speaking and listening activities, group times, teacher read-alouds, looking at books, and the informal nature of children's conversations as they draw and write.)

- The committee decides to identify dramatic play as a central element of the prekindergarten literacy curriculum. (For example, Standard 1, Language for Information and Understanding, and Standard 4, Social Interaction, are both basic aspects of children's imaginative play.)

- Lastly, the committee identifies additional specific elements of early childhood literacy curriculum with the knowledge that, while remaining natural and meaningful in content, most elements will address multiple state literacy standards as mandated by this state.

The committee examines a number of behaviors that help develop literacy in young children (Wilford 1998; 2000; 2003) and how those behaviors correlate to the state standards, including the following:

- reading behaviors

- phonemic awareness

- oral language

- concepts of print

- word recognition

- letter identification and phonics principles

- connections between pictures and words

- early writing

- comprehension and the concept of story

Reading Behaviors (Standards 1 and 3)

Children will have access to a wide range of trade books, invitingly displayed and relevant to their interests. They will be able to look at books independently and be read to on a daily basis by their teacher. Through observing their independent examination of books, teachers will note how frequently each child chooses to look at a book from the classroom library, whether the child holds the book upside down or right side up, and whether the pages are turned from right to left or from left to right.

Phonemic Awareness (Standards 1 through 4)

Songs, rhymes, and chants are all opportunities for children to play with the sounds of language and develop phonemic sensitivity. Many of these rhymes and songs are requested by children themselves; for instance, "Twinkle, Twinkle Little Star" contains sets of rhyming words that sound the same—star/are, high/sky—even though they don't look the same in written form. Because the words rhyme, they are predictable. Rhyming helps children anticipate the word that will come next in a phrase or a sentence. This is helpful and enjoyable literacy practice for children, giving them a strategy to apply to written language.

Oral Language (Standards 1 through 4)

Imaginative-play scenes where children can challenge each other's actions, words, and meanings are vitally important as a fertile ground for language growth, both contextual and semantic. A designated place for play with graphic and written symbols is also an important addition to children's literacy growth as they engage in interactive talk, such as in the following example.

> KATHRYN: William! Are you making a rainbow?
> WILLIAM: Yes! How did you know?
> KATHRYN: Because it's got all the colors in it.
> WILLIAM: What are you making?
> KATHRYN: The ABCDEFGs and the numbers. You know, the song ABCDEFG. . . .

Working with other children in a relaxed atmosphere, one in which children are not mandated to sit in specific places, allows for dynamic and interactive literacy learning. When children help each other or sit next to each other, there's a real sense of companionship in a literacy activity that minimizes difficulty.

Concepts of Print (Standard 2)

Many young children make early connections to reading through their experiments with writing, although when and how they become interested will vary. Long before children can formally read and write, they will engage in time-honored acts of imitation (which adults call "pretending"). Imagine two four-year-olds. One is making a series of marks that flow conventionally from left to right. The other is turning the pages of a picture book and pointing to them in sequence. Both of these children have made the basic connections between the way print moves across a page and the way a story progresses through a book. They understand that directionality—the movement of print and pictures from the left to the right side of the page—is a basic convention of literacy in our culture.

Word Recognition (Standards 1 through 3)

Children are natural detectives and primed to bring meaning to print. Knowing that the car stops at the stop sign—and understanding what it means to stop—invests the sign with a message. The sign on the guinea pig cage at school, "Our guinea pig," has the same effect. A reading detective also notes that there are not only pictures in a picture book, but also pages with black squiggles on them. Preschool children may already know that these black squiggles are words by being read to. The next step is to connect the squiggles with the meaning of a story as they notice similarities and differences. Once children understand these concepts of print, they will begin to identify individual words in the text. If we look at Margaret Wise Brown's *Goodnight Moon* (1947), the inner dialogue or thought process may go something like this:

> I know that the word "goodnight" comes here . . . (flip) and here . . . (flip) and here! It's a long word when you say it. Maybe it looks long too. Well, this word is long, and it starts with the letter "g" like "go. Go . . . goodnight." That must mean "goodnight!" (*Before long the reading detective has added all the words on the pages starting with the word "goodnight" to her reading vocabulary.*) This has to say "room" because it comes with the picture for the Goodnight room . . . and this says "moon" . . . and this says "cow" . . . and "light" . . . and "bears"!

Letter Identification and Phonics Principles (Standards 1, 3, and 4)

Children learn a great deal about phonics from their own early writing efforts, but teachers can introduce and expand phonics principles during group work that invites children's participation. In the following example, teacher Sonna works with her kindergartners on the letters and letter sounds "w" and "wh," standing in front of an easel with paper attached. The children are sitting on the floor in a group and call out words with the letter "w" in them for her to record. The mood is calm; the tone is one of complete engagement.

MICHAEL: When!

SONNA: "When" (writing it down) . . . that starts with a "wh." You don't hear it, but you can feel it if you say it on the back your hand. Let's all try. When . . . when . . . feel the "wh"?

CHILDREN: YES!!

LAILANY: Went!

SONNA: Would you like "went," Lailany? (writing it down) I went to school this morning. Did everyone give me a word? Anna?

ANNA: I can't think of a word.

SONNA: Wait a minute—you just said one! "Word"! (writing it down) Now, if I put an "l" here, between the "r" and the "d," what will I have?

CHILDREN: World!

CHARLEY: I've got another word . . . way!

SONNA: "Way." Which *way* do we go? How much do you *weigh?* (writes both words down) Why does it sound the same, but we can spell it different ways to mean different things? I don't really know myself.

DEVIN: Willy Wonka!

SONNA: (writing "Willy Wonka") Why am I beginning these words with uppercase letters?

CHILDREN: Because they're names!

After the lesson the children disperse eagerly to work on the letter "w" in their journals, adding words and pictures in the spaces provided.

Connections between Pictures and Words (Standards 1 and 3)

Most children paint, scribble, and draw as naturally as they play long before they attempt to write words. As they paint and draw, they are experimenting with issues of control—"If I move the marker this way, what kind of line will it make?" "If I want to draw a face, what sort of shape will I get if the brush goes this way?" Drawing pictures is the logical beginning place for the development of hand-eye coordination, and provides meaningful fine-motor-skill practice. Allowing and encouraging children to draw set the literacy process in motion. As children begin to draw pictures of things they see or think about, they are tapping into the fundamental understanding that the marks they are making on paper are a picture of something else. For instance, the child knows that the tree he has drawn is not really a tree, but a picture that means "tree."

Early Writing (Standards 1 through 4)

Letters are seen by children as lines, straight and curved. With this realization comes the understanding that by putting these lines (or letters) together, you can form words. Learning to write is much more than letter formation. Young children deliberately explore written language through experimentation, sometimes turning letters into drawings and shaping them in different ways. Some children love to practice making letters and will do so for long periods of time. Others will have uncertain pencil grips and struggle to conquer letters like B, D, P, Q, and S, but all children can be encouraged at each stage of their writing development. As children search for meaning in print, they often want to write their names. Other words soon follow such as "dog" and "cat," and the names of family members. Children who are allowed and encouraged to experiment will begin to write words using letters that represent the most prominent consonant sounds they hear, along with some short and long vowel sounds. This kind of inventive spelling is an important step toward eventual conventional spelling. As handwriting improves (remembering that improvement is an individual process), children are motivated toward legibility in direct relationship to the desire for their work to be read by others. Older children naturally enjoy working together as writers, editors, and illustrators if the classroom environment allows for this kind of interaction.

Comprehension and the Concept of Story (Standards 1 through 4)

Every event of every day in our lives is a story. Stories in books contain the potential for making significant connections between children's life experiences, their developmental stages, and the pages of print. Every book holds some aspect of story within its covers. For young children, the story draws in the listener with familiar events and enthralling pictures. As they listen to adults read aloud, children add their own associations and feelings to a book. In the process, new vocabulary is introduced, and listeners begin to incorporate the concepts of beginning, middle, and end. Early writers love to read their stories aloud to classmates. Children who are tentative about attempting to write enjoy having their stories and ideas written down by interested adults. As teachers encourage children to dictate, they are able to tell much longer and more fluent stories than their emergent writing skills might otherwise allow. Telling stories, using puppets, and acting out plays based on folktales or the children's own stories are other avenues for helping children internalize concepts of story.

The Assessment Process

Confident that they can meet state literacy standards through the identification of appropriate early childhood curriculum opportunities and teaching, the committee outlines an assessment process that will honor each child's literacy progress. Teachers are asked to keep individual literacy portfolios for every child in the class. The portfolios will include

- drawings and writing efforts dated from earliest to latest

- digital photographs of paintings

- digital photographs of the child engaged in literacy behaviors

- teacher observations of the child engaging in as many aspects of the literacy curriculum as possible

Looking from top to bottom, we see that state curriculum standards can be thought through to preserve their intent while maintaining early learning standards, respect for young children's individual dispositions, and appropriate early childhood practice. The teacher-caregiver's work runs the gamut from setting up a learning environment to nurturing her early childhood community. Acting as coach and leader, she leaves plenty of time for imaginative play and curriculum choices, thus enabling opportunities for one-on-one attention as well as interactive group times.

PROFESSIONAL DEVELOPMENT SUGGESTIONS

Use a selection of the following books on a wide variety of curriculum areas, published or copublished by NAEYC, to examine, validate, and enrich your practice as you ask yourself how state standards are addressed. As you introduce new material or implement an activity or project, keep a journal of successes along with notes regarding ideas that did not work as well. Make time for sharing your observations and discoveries with colleagues.

Early Childhood Curriculum: A Bibliography

Colker, Laura J. 2005. *The cooking book: Fostering young children's learning and delight*. Washington, D.C.: NAEYC.

Copley, Juanita V. 2000. *The young child and mathematics*. Washington, DC: NAEYC; Reston, VA: National Council of Teachers of Mathematics.

Engel, Brenda S. 1995. *Considering children's art: Why and how to value their work*. Washington, DC: NAEYC.

Gadzikowski, Ann. 2007. *Story dictation: A guide for early childhood professionals*. St. Paul: Redleaf Press.

Helm, Judy Harris, and Sallee Beneke, eds. 2003. *The Power of projects: Meeting contemporary challenges in early childhood classrooms—strategies and solutions*. Early Childhood Education Series. New York: Teachers College Press; Washington, DC: NAEYC.

Hirsch, Elisabeth S., ed. 1996. *The block book*. 3rd edition. Washington, DC: NAEYC.

Jones, Elizabeth, and John Nimmo. 1994. *Emergent curriculum*. Washington, DC: NAEYC.

McDonald, Dorothy T. 1979. *Music in our lives: The early years*. Washington, DC: NAEYC.

Owocki, Gretchen. 2001. *Make way for literacy! Teaching the way young children learn*. Portsmouth, NH: Heinemann.

Rivkin, Mary S. 1995. *The great outdoors: Restoring children's right to play outside*. Washington, DC: NAEYC.

Schickedanz, Judith A., and Renée M. Casbergue. 2004. *Writing in preschool: Learning to orchestrate meaning and marks*. Newark, DE: International Reading Association.

Stacey, Susan. 2009. *Emergent curriculum in early childhood settings: From theory to practice*. St. Paul: Redleaf Press.

Vance, Emily, and Patricia Jiménez Weaver. 2002. *Class meetings: Young children solving problems together*. Washington, DC: NAEYC.

Worth, Karen, and Sharon Grollman. 2003. *Worms, shadows, and whirlpools: Science in the early childhood classroom*. Portsmouth, NH: Heinemann; Newton, MA: EDC; Washington, DC: NAEYC.

Chapter 8

Helping Families Support Children's Learning

The phrase "parents as partners" is central to the mission of every early childhood program I know. Without a partnership between home and school, children are left to cope with different messages that are difficult to figure out and internalize. This does not mean, however, that the goal of a strong family-school relationship is easy to achieve. Although developing strong bonds with the families in our centers and schools is a priority, reaching the reality takes reflection, practice, and skills that come with time.

Balancing Warmth and Professionalism

It's almost impossible for most of us to like every person we meet. Some children are harder for adults to like than others, and that goes for their family members as well. In my experience, I've found that often the most complex and challenging children are those I eventually feel closest to. Working with their families can be a lot harder. As a director, out of the classroom and missing the rewards of working with individual children in a classroom community, I had to develop some guidelines and approaches for my staff to use in their work with families. I had to simultaneously brace myself to accept that the buck stops at my office, no matter how busy I am or how angry the parent or staff person is! Working together as a staff, we discussed central issues of warmth and professionalism, resulting in consensus on the following approaches.

Consciously determine the importance of warmth. This includes tone of voice, a projected sense of comfort, knowledge of the child in question, and the ability to reach out sympathetically if you sense a need for support. At the same time, remember that you are a professional teacher-caregiver or director with knowledge of the developing child and insights based on day-to-day contact. Although some parents or families may be more difficult than others, it's important for you to treat all people equally. For example, accepting personal invitations from some parents or families but not from others is a no-no, as is demonstrating your likes or dislikes through facial expressions such as smiling at some people more than others, rolling your eyes, or ignoring certain parents or caregivers altogether.

In the event that a parent or family member causes you to feel under attack, realize immediately that the onslaught is not personal. It almost always relates to the individual's vulnerability in connection with his or her own stress or worry about the child. This is really hard to do, but just listening until the barrage of words is at an end will send a message in itself. Take a deep inner breath, hold your anger in a separate place (in other words, don't let it get to your stomach), and at the same time focus on listening carefully. When you respond, do so objectively and without anger. Let your steady voice take the issues raised back to conversational mode.

Maintaining Structure in Your Relationships with Families

The section of this book on communicating with families in chapter 6 details the importance of a sound separation policy. Entry into early childhood education settings provides unique opportunities to establish strong relationships with parents as they entrust to teacher-caregivers their child's safety and overall well-being. Every school or center will have a slightly different policy, and every family will have a somewhat differing approach, but a family's central question remains the same: "How will you care for my child as an individual and nurture his (or her) disposition to learn?" A structured yet responsive approach to separation is the foundation of trust. The confidence you build with families in these initial days will become the basis of warm yet professional continuing relationships.

Off-the-Cuff Responses

Beware of off-the-cuff responses to daily inquiries by the family of a particular child. This creates a situation that is unhelpful for the child and also sometimes misleading for the adult. For instance, if you have a real concern that you anticipate raising in a family-teacher conference, daily reports can be easily misinterpreted as "everything's okay," and your efforts to make a referral will be undermined. Provide structure by being direct, and even use a touch of humor as you respond with a generality such as "I love teaching this class of threes!" or "Looking for a daily report, are you? It's much more rewarding to save our observations and questions for the conference. Did you sign up for a time yet?" Of course if you detect persistent anxiety, a mini-conference or phone call may be in order.

Availability

Teacher-caregivers have a range of personal as well as professional demands to deal with, so establishing an availability policy that everyone agrees to lends a sense of stability and structure to the program. Directors and staff can determine the policy together, depending on family needs and practical constraints. Some programs that have a high proportion of single parents, families below the poverty line, and parents holding down multiple jobs may find it difficult to bring families in for regular conferences. If this is the case, then outreach is necessary. Some possibilities include

- frequent written communications home (if possible in both English and Spanish or the language of origin of many in the program)

- journals that travel between home and school

- conferences scheduled in the early morning or at the end of the day

- an exchange of telephone numbers

All of the above put additional pressure on staff, but should be considered, along with other possibilities, to maintain viable partnerships.

If conferences are a feasible avenue for the program, their timing and structure will lend a feeling of continuity. At least two conferences, one in the fall and one in the spring, should be scheduled. The fall conferences allows for an initial "intake" meeting where the teacher-caregiver asks for family input. The teacher-caregiver should also be prepared to answer questions related to program philosophy and assessment strategies. A conference later in the year allows teacher-caregivers to share examples of progress and to raise issues of possible concern. Allowing substantial time, especially for families of the youngest children or those who present concerns, is wise. On the other hand, having a clear time limit in mind is helpful as long as the conclusion is not abrupt.

Reporting to Families

Reporting to families of young children in an educational climate of standardized assessments and testing means that we must be able to show individual strengths and personal progress in a convincing way. It's not enough to tell the truth about the unreliability and negative effects of testing in early childhood. Early childhood educators must help families understand their children's progress through multiple avenues that illuminate the many ways that children learn.

Consider the power of messages conveyed through the environment, such as mounting children's artwork on classroom and hallway walls. The old adage "a picture is worth a thousand words" has some merit, and now it's possible to use technology to enrich the images, adding digital photographs of children building with blocks, using manipulative materials, engaging in dramatic play, and displaying reading behaviors in the classroom library. Framing the images with construction paper helps to set them off in a professional way.

Individual portfolios of children's work are powerful, because they demonstrate progress over time. When pieces of work are too big or bulky to save, or the child is adamant about taking work home, a digital camera can come to the rescue. Photographing the child in action provides documentation of a range of interactive activities and learning experiences, as does videotaping if it's available. One teacher I know uses a computer to store files of children's work so that during a conference families can view the work online and discuss the child's growth with him in the process.

Conducting a Descriptive Review of a Child (as described in chapter 5) is another meaningful way to bring families into the documentation process. Descriptive reviews take time to prepare, and not every family will want to participate. But once they are experienced, word will spread about the empowering nature of looking at children's strengths through this lens.

Some early childhood programs find that including the young child in a conference has merit. When children are old enough to know what's going on, looking at their work in an ongoing way and seeing their own progress can provide a tremendous surge of self-confidence. It's also a helpful technique for including a child in finding the solution to a problem or adding a new goal. For example, the teacher-caregiver or parent might say, "Tell us what you think happened when you got in the fight with Jimmy" or "Is there a particular piece of work you like? Why? (or don't like? Why?) What could we do at school (or home) to help?" Conferences that include family and child, though potentially fruitful, should not mean that the adults in the child's life have no other means of communicating. Families of young children invariably need adult one-on-one time as well.

Dealing with Frequently Asked Questions

Some issues are higher on the list of today's families' priorities than others. The most frequent challenges I have encountered focus on the place of dramatic play in the program, methods of teaching literacy, the role of technology, and the meaning of "the basics."

"Children Seem to Be Just Playing at School All Day Long! When Are They Going to Learn?"

As described in chapters 1 and 3, children's dramatic play is one of the foundations of learning. Children become comfortable with symbolic processes as they learn, for instance, that one play prop can stand in for another. The foundation for children's understanding of abstract concepts is built from their repeated, spontaneous efforts to pretend, to see one object as symbolic of something else. Playground activity also invites symbolic play, simultaneously building coordination and large-muscle dexterity. Imaginative play, a natural, primary tool young children employ as they grow and develop, is key to the formation of social relationships as well.

To summarize, if children are denied access to what they do instinctively and imaginatively, their attitude toward school will suffer, as will their ability to relate to others. In learning to understand the basics of play and its central place in curriculum, families can be helped to see that the formation of positive relationships and the ability to use one's imagination in later life are central to future success and individual fulfillment.

"When Will My Child Learn to Read?"

Experts tell us that children most often learn to read independently between the ages of five and seven. Just as in learning to talk, learning to read is an individual process that will unfold over time. There are many preliminary signs of early reading to be noticed:

- recognizing occasional letters and words on signs and labels

- experimenting with writing

- looking at books for pleasure and turning pages

- using the pictures to tell the story

By the time a child enters kindergarten, he or she may have acquired enough skills to read independently. However, it is more common that five-year-olds are not at this level of reading development. Parents can assist by sharing books and recipes at home, encouraging reading and writing efforts, taking down a dictated letter as the child's "scribe" and then reading it back, and playing with magnetic or wooden letters as the child begins to show interest in their sounds.

Reading aloud is important because it inspires children of all ages to enter the world of literacy. The closeness you experience when reading aloud helps to enhance your child's self-esteem, creates a positive connection to books, and provides motivation to discover the content between the covers.

Memorizing the words that go on the same page as the picture is not "just memorizing" but a logical progression to making connections between spoken words and the words on a page. Pointing to words as the story progresses is sometimes the child's efficient way to focus on a specific word without impeding the meaning of the story (Wilford 1998).

Finally, let your child catch you in the act of reading. Family reading times, when everyone chooses a book, magazine, or (for the adults) newspaper or work-related reading, will help your child to see the value of print in many forms—for all ages.

"Technology Is Here to Stay. What Role Does It Play in My Child's School Experience?"

While acknowledging some positive uses of technology for young children, the American Academy of Pediatrics and the Alliance for Childhood have called for a moratorium on increased use of television and computers in homes and schools. They cite possible dangers if young children are encouraged to be passive rather than active learners. This is an important caution, challenging us to assess technology usage from a developmentally appropriate standpoint. Let's not fool ourselves into thinking that interacting with a computer is identical to interacting with another human being. A computer may "speak," but it does not speak as humans do—asking questions, spontaneously responding or laughing. It does not encourage gross-motor movement or provide the sensory stimulation of discovering the properties of wet and dry sand or the amazement of creating a new paint color by mixing two primary colors together. Nor does a computer deliver the physics principles gained from constructing an intricate block building. Computer software designed for practice or problem solving may have value as an additional tool, but only as one of many choices in an early childhood classroom that nurtures the individual child's disposition to learn.

The ages of the children and consideration of developmental readiness in context of the whole child are important guides in making decisions about appropriate uses of technology in an early childhood classroom, so keep the following in mind—the younger the child, the less important it is to supply technological resources and the more important it is to provide all the classic materials of early childhood. Dress-ups, manipulatives, art materials, and picture books are crucial for social, emotional, intellectual, and physical development. For example, computer programs that mimic art experiences can supplement but should never replace the textural, sensory interactions with paper and paint, crayons, markers, oil pastels, and chalk, which foster children's imagination and symbolic thinking.

Abstract concepts develop slowly. Older fours and fives are beginning to grasp the idea of cause and effect. Problem-solving computer programs for youngsters of this age are okay, while programs focusing on drill and practice of number concepts, word recognition, and letter-sound correlation are just that—drill and practice. Computer programs and some Internet sites that explore social studies or environmental themes, geared for the appropriate ages and interests of prekindergarten or kindergarten children, can be useful resources.

"Do You Focus on 'The Basics'?"

Today's early childhood professionals have the task of helping families change the way they think about "the basics." Families are sometimes overwhelmed by messages touted by the media (and by some current educational policy makers) that may mislead them into believing that standards are somehow achieved by a dry mental process and rote practice. As professionals who work with children on a daily basis, we know this is not true. We know it's not true because of our personal experience, the findings of decades of research in developmental psychology and education, and current understandings gained from brain imaging.

We know that children are active learners, individual meaning-makers who acquire knowledge in multiple ways. This applies to children who struggle with developmental delays and other challenges as much as it applies to those who are seen as progressing on a normal developmental path. The only differences lie in the rate of progress, the accommodations that may be necessary, and the sometimes-subtle task of discovering the interests, possibilities, and strengths of children with special needs.

When families understand that their children can and will develop and learn, anxiety recedes, and confidence in their ability to nurture is strengthened. Early childhood professionals have a responsibility to help families relax and consider the *real* basics. For instance, we can convey the idea that capitalizing on natural opportunities to communicate is a primary teaching strategy in fostering children's growth. Adults need only look to the normal routines of their lives to be encouraged in that first imperative—talking to and with their children. In non–English-speaking households, families can be empowered by the knowledge that conversing in their home language will help build strong vocabularies and thinking skills. Singing songs and playing with rhyming words in any language attune children's ears to subtle rhythms and sounds of language. Reading to and with children may be more natural for some families than others, but telling stories is an equally powerful act in the development of a sense of story and interest in literacy. A few props in a relaxed atmosphere can do wonders in allowing for symbolic processes to flourish, as Gunther Kress describes so well in making connections between the symbolic acts of pretending and literacy development:

> In learning to read and write, children come as thoroughly experienced makers of signs in any medium that is at hand. . . . [There is a] wide range of media which they employ as a matter of course—toys and constructions of various kinds; Lego blocks; cardboard boxes; blankets; chairs; corners of rooms; pens and paper; scissors, paste, and paper. . . . The form and the material of the signs made by children are for them expressive of the meanings which they intend to make. . . . Say children want to play "camping" in a room in their house, and they need a "tent." Blankets and bedcovers provide the material. . . . Or they want to play "pirates" and therefore need a "pirate ship." A cardboard box provides a container, in which they can sit, it serves as the "vessel" and the carpet as the "ocean." (Kress 1997, 8–9)

Families are our partners in the endeavor to nurture all young children's disposition to learn. Mutual confidence and children's self-confidence are our goals. Interaction rather than instruction is the means to real learning in early childhood, although it will never be an easy job to convince those who were schooled in a traditional top-down way that this is so.

Reaching families through their inner desire for and clarity concerning children's social, emotional, and mental growth is sometimes the key—and often a key we overlook because it's so simple. To reach for the key, we can ask these questions of ourselves and of them: "Is your child happy to come to school?" "Is your child joyful?" If the answers are no, we have work to do. If the answers are yes, then we will still have work to do.

And what wonderful work it is.

PROFESSIONAL DEVELOPMENT SUGGESTIONS

Most families are eager to learn more about their children's school lives, even if time is scarce. As a staff, plan and invite families to participate in a hands-on workshop in the classrooms, hear a guest speaker talking about an issue of current interest (child development, safety, setting limits), or participate in a storytelling session. Provide a simple meal for the children, who can stay with volunteer staff, and light refreshments for the adult—thus no babysitting required. Early evenings after work are often the best choice for a parent event.

In collaboration with the director and a teacher committee, brainstorm with families about a project they might like to undertake with children and staff. Saturdays work well for gardening or planting, a building project (perhaps a piece of simple climbing equipment or classroom furniture), or a book fair. Divide planning responsibilities, but give autonomy to families in carrying out the project.

Epilogue

As I come to the end of this book, it feels like the end of an adventure. But, I tell myself that life is an adventure. Being an early childhood teacher-caregiver, director of an early childhood program, elementary school teacher, or teacher educator is an adventure. Sometimes we feel under-valued, even unrecognized. We are not yet compensated fairly for what we do, although what we do is undoubtedly the most people-intensive work around. Still, those of us fortunate enough to work with children have an advantage over many in our society. We have rewards others do not, in-cluding a constant connection to what it means to be human. We experi-ence humor, joy alongside pain, and a centeredness that working with or near children brings us nearly every day.

Most importantly, as those directly on the line with our emotions, we have the opportunity to feel deeply, to laugh with true enjoyment, and to watch our work yield positive results before our eyes. Teaching young chil-dren, being privileged to nurture their growth, is quite simply one of the best professions in the world.

References

Ashton-Warner, Sylvia. 1986. *Teacher*. New York: Simon & Schuster.

Ballenger, Cynthia. 1999. *Teaching other people's children: Literacy and learning in a bilingual classroom*. New York: Teachers College Press.

Biber, Barbara. 1984. *Early education and psychological development*. New Haven, CT: Yale University Press.

Bowman, Barbara T., and Evelyn K. Moore. 2006. *School readiness and social-emotional development: Perspectives on cultural diversity*. Washington, DC: National Black Child Development Institute.

Brosterman, Norman, and Kiyoshi Togashi. 1997. *Inventing kindergarten*. New York: H. N. Abrams.

Brown, Margaret Wise. 1947. *Goodnight moon*. New York: Harper.

Carini, Patricia F. 1979. *The art of seeing and the visibility of the person*. Grand Forks: University of North Dakota.

Carson, Rachel. 1962. *Silent spring*. Boston: Houghton Mifflin.

———. 1965. *The sense of wonder*. New York: Harper & Row.

Casper, Virginia, and Steven B. Schultz. 1999. *Gay parents/straight schools: Building communication and trust*. New York: Teachers College Press.

Clay, Marie M. 1991. *Becoming literate: The construction of inner control*. Portsmouth, NH: Heinemann.

Comer, James P. 1997. *Waiting for a miracle: Why schools can't solve our problems—and how we can*. New York: Dutton.

Committee on Integrating the Science of Early Childhood Development. 2000. *From neurons to neighborhoods: The science of early childhood development*. Washington, DC: National Research Council Institute of Medicine.

Crain, William. 2005. *Theories of development: Concepts and applications.* 5th edition. Upper Saddle River, NJ: Prentice Hall.

Delpit, Lisa D. 1995. *Other people's children: Cultural conflict in the classroom.* New York: New Press.

Edwards, Carolyn P., and Carlina Rinaldi. 2008. *The diary of Laura: Perspectives on a Reggio Emilia diary.* St. Paul: Redleaf Press.

Ewald, Carl, 1924. *My little boy.* Translated by Alexander Teixeira de Mattos. New York: Scribner.

Fassler, Rebekah. 2003. *Room for talk: Teaching and learning in a multilingual kindergarten.* New York: Teachers College Press.

Froebel, Friedrich. 1982. Froebel 1782–1852. In *Three thousand years of educational wisdom: Selections from the great documents,* ed. R. Ulich, 523–76. Cambridge, MA: Harvard University Press.

Gardner, Howard. 1983. *Frames of mind: The theory of multiple intelligences.* New York: Basic Books.

———. 1999. *Intelligence reframed: Multiple intelligences for the twenty-first century.* New York: Basic Books.

———. 2006. *Multiple intelligences: New horizons.* New York: Basic Books.

Greenspan, Stanley I., Sheila Hanna, and Sara Wilford. 1990. *Floor time: Tuning in to each child.* Video. New York: Scholastic.

Gronlund, Gaye. 2006. *Make early learning standards come alive: Connecting your practice and curriculum to state guidelines.* St. Paul: Redleaf Press.

Hawthorne, Nathaniel. 2003. *Twenty days with Julian and Little Bunny by Papa.* New York: New York Review of Books.

Heubert, Jay Philip, and Robert Mason Hauser, eds. 1999. *High stakes: Testing for tracking, promotion, and graduation.* Washington, DC: National Academy Press.

Hilgers, Laura. 2006. The best in kids' education. *Child Magazine,* September.

Himley, Margaret, and Patricia F. Carini. 2000. *From another angle: Children's strengths and school standards: The Prospect Center's descriptive review of the child.* New York: Teachers College Press.

Katz, Lilian. 1987. Early education: What should young children be doing? In *Early schooling: The national debate,* ed. S. L. Kagan and E. F. Zigler, 151–67. New Haven, CT: Yale University Press.

Kress, Gunther R. 1997. *Before writing: Rethinking the paths to literacy.* New York: Routlege.

Mitchell, Lucy Sprague, and Sam Brian. 1991. *Young geographers: How they explore the world and how they map the world.* New York: Bank Street College of Education.

Moffitt, John. 2003. To look at any thing. In *Teaching with fire: Poetry that sustains the courage to teach*, ed. S. M. Intrator and M. Scribner, 125. San Francisco: Jossey-Bass.

Morrison, Toni. 1997. *The dancing mind: Speech upon acceptance of the National Book Foundation Medal for Distinguished Contribution to American Letters on the sixth of November, Nineteen hundred and ninety-six.* New York: Alfred A. Knopf.

National Association for the Education of Young Children, and the National Association of Early Childhood Specialists in State Departments of Education. 2002. *Early learning standards: Creating the conditions for success.* Washington, DC: NAEYC.

Painter, Nell Irvin. 2006. *Creating Black Americans: African-American history and its meanings, 1619 to the present.* New York: Oxford University Press.

Paley, Vivian Gussin. 2000. *White teacher.* Cambridge, MA: Harvard University Press.

PBS Home Video. 1997. *Scientific American Frontiers: Pieces of Mind.* VHS. Washington, DC: PBS.

Piaget, Jean, and Bärbel Inhelder. 1969. *The psychology of the child.* New York: Basic Books.

Polakow, Valerie. 1993. *Lives on the edge: Single mothers and their children in the other America.* Chicago: University of Chicago Press.

Rogoff, Barbara. 2003. *The cultural nature of human development.* New York: Oxford University Press.

Shore, Rima. 1997. *Rethinking the brain: New insights into early development.* New York: Families and Work Institute.

Snow, Catherine E., Peg Griffin, and M. Susan Burns. 2005. *Knowledge to support the teaching of reading: Preparing teachers for a changing world.* San Francisco: Jossey-Bass.

Wells, C. Gordon. 1986. *The meaning makers: Children learning language and using language to learn.* Portsmouth, NH: Heinemann.

Wilford, Sara. 1998. *What you need to know when your child is learning to read.* New York: Scholastic.

———. 2000. From play to literacy: Implications for the classroom. Occasional Paper Series. New York: Sarah Lawrence College Child Development Institute.

———. 2003. *From pictures to words.* New York: Sarah Lawrence College Child Development Institute.

Zigler, Edward F., Matia Finn-Stevenson, and Nancy W. Hall. 2002. *The first three years and beyond: Brain development and social policy.* New Haven, CT: Yale University Press.